Blessing Leaders

144 blessings to pray over leaders to transform society

Collette Vosloo

collette@wordjourneys.co.za; collettevosloo1@gmail.com

Cover design: Teboho Ntsamai
Cover image (Shutterstock): The ripples of wise and unwise leadership are evident in every society. It is God, through His immeasurable grace and generosity, who adds wisdom to leaders who seek it, causing them to be life-giving to the many levels of diversity in their spheres of influence.

Language editing: Hadassah Dannhauser

Printed in South Africa
Group 7 Drukkers en Uitgewers BK
www.groep7.co.za

First print 2016
ISBN 978-0-620-70858-6
Second print 2019
ISBN 978-0-620-82650-1
e-Book
ISBN 978-0-620-82651-8

Also available:
Word journeys: A collection of poems encompassing authentic expressions of worship, questions from an imperfect being to Perfection, and glimpses of God's commitment to see His children rise up in their full, God-given potential.

Acknowledgements

Firstly, all honour and glory to God for this book – for His prompting, direction and revelation. Father, You really made a way where there was none, and again I am amazed by Your omniscience and kindness. Secondly, my heartfelt appreciation to the friends who prayed this book into being. Specifically, Annette, Celia, Helena, Hermana, Ina, Jansie, Karen, Louise, Marelize, Mariska, Mimi, Natasja and Trudie – thank you for being part of what God wants to release in this season.

Contents

Foreword

Not all leaders are in a position of authority of their own volition. Many of the people who are expected to provide guidance to fellow earth dwellers would gladly relinquish their leadership position to more suitable candidates, in their estimation.

Leadership, no matter how insignificant in scope, will always be a great challenge as one of its main tenets is the responsibility for very diverse human beings. In these modern times leaders are often and constantly criticised, or dismantled by social opinion. Our media has normalised the disrespect doled out to leaders, and it is a rare occurrence for any applause to be given to those who actually succeed in accomplishing their aims while being life giving to their followers.

In such an environment, few leaders are able to attain to the myriad expectations thrust on them. None of us is able to improve our leaders. We cannot force them to become more sensible and wholesome in their abilities and character.

We must recognise that God alone appoints whomever He wills (Daniel 4:17 and 5:21). The writer of the book of Hebrews, a leader in the New Testament Church himself, starts Hebrews 13:18 with these words: "Pray for us…". This duty is confirmed in Paul's word to Timothy to pray for all in positions of authority (1 Timothy 2:2).

Through this book Collette provides us with practical tools, and many insights on how to bless and pray for leaders. We are given Scriptural understanding about the intricacies of righteous leadership. As the standard of authentic leadership unfolds before us we have the opportunity to sow powerful seeds of blessing over the individuals that shape our lives. In faith we expect that these seeds will soon germinate and mature our leaders to excel in the godly fulfilment of their catalytic roles in our society.

Our opinions will never accomplish the change our communities need. Our voicing the truths of the Father over countless influential people, will. His Word will never return void, but will accomplish and prosper in the thing for which He sent it (Isaiah 55:11).

Will you take up this tool and become part of the army that invests into the spiritual dimension, so that we can see an upsurge of upright, exemplary leaders?

Leon Coetzee
Director: Unlimited Prayer Frontiers South Africa
(Incorporating the Academy of Prayer)
www.upfsa.co.za

Introduction

Effective leadership is important. You know it. I know it. Every leadership guru knows it, and everyone either blossoming or wilting under leadership knows it. At the time of revising this book, Amazon had more than 60 000 titles on leadership available. Just Google, "What makes a good leader?" and take your pick from more than a billion results.

Leadership matters. Life-giving leadership matters.

I have a soft spot for leaders. While I do not believe we should put any leader on a pedestal – a world of harm has come from elevating leaders to god-like status – leaders should also not be slighted.

Leadership is a lonely position. Lonely in the sense that when all is said and done, the buck stops at the top. It is also lonely because many leaders lack the proper support from the next level of leaders or management, or worse, do not trust their support.

Of course, leadership has its joys – charting new territory, achieving goals, or seeing people reach their potential.

That said, what I think, especially where this book is concerned, does not really matter. What matters is that God has this leadership thing covered. Thoroughly. And why wouldn't He – isn't He the consummate Leader?

Godly instruction

He values leaders. So much so, that He, through Paul, commands us in 1 Timothy 2:1-4 to pray for leadership:

Therefore I exhort first of all that supplications, prayers, intercessions,- giving of thanks be made for all men, for kings-all who are in authority, that we may lead a quiet-peaceable life in all godliness and reverence. For this is good and acceptable in the sight of God our Savior, who desires all men to be saved-to come to the knowledge of the truth.

Did you notice? "… that we may lead a quiet-peaceable life in all godliness and reverence". Are you living a peaceful and quiet life? There are few places on earth today that fit that description.

Solomon knew a thing or two about leadership:

When the righteous are in authority, the people rejoice; but when a wicked man rules, the people groan. (Proverbs 29:2)

And, for emphasis, hear Habakkuk's lamentation:

Why do You show me iniquity, and cause me to see trouble? For plundering-violence are before me; there is strife, and contention arises. Therefore the law is powerless, and justice never goes forth. For the wicked surround the righteous; Therefore perverse judgment proceeds. (Habakkuk 1:3-4)

Interesting. The law is powerless. Justice is ineffectual. The Amplified version says that justice is perverted. Destruction and violence rule. The wicked surround the righteous. Peace? Not much. At the time of Habakkuk's writing, God was preparing to use the Chaldeans to punish Judah. Why? Because the leaders were oppressing the poor.

When the wicked are multiplied, transgression increases; but the righteous will see their fall. (Proverbs 29:16)

Get the picture?

Leaders, whether due to their influence, or because God determined it to be that way (probably both), establish the spiritual direction of their followers.

If we are to enjoy peace, righteousness must reign. For righteousness to reign, our leaders must be transformed. For leaders to be transformed, we have to lift them up before God – without first siding with the accuser of the brethren (Revelation 12:10) by complaining, gossiping, or cursing.

Our responsibility

I had a hard time understanding why so few prayers for those in authority seemed to hit the mark. God, gracious teacher that He is, took me on a journey through the somewhat murky world of our motives. Why did we pray the way we did? What lay behind some of the very eloquent petitions for godly leaders? And then this scripture:

You ask and do not receive, because you ask amiss, that you may spend it on your pleasures. (James 4:3)

But does this not only refer to material things? Perhaps. However, if I am praying, for example, for my nation's leaders because I feel threatened, my motive is fear-based (and I have no love because love and fear cannot co-exist – 1 John 4:18). If my sole focus in praying for my boss is to ask for wisdom to make the right decision about my promotion, it is all about me. If I am praying for strategy for the city leaders to deal with the increasing number of destitute people, is my concern really about the poor, or about my discomfort at having to face them (and perhaps even my reluctance to help them)? The agenda? Unrighteous. My prayers? Unanswered.

This book is by no means the definitive guide to blessing leadership, but it's a good start.

About the book

This book focuses on the nation of Israel and its walk with God prior to the birth of Jesus. God spent hundreds of years helping His chosen people cast off the bondage of slavery. He taught them up close and personal about the ways He wanted them to draw close to Him (and live). He gave pertinent instructions to their leaders and not only established those in authority, but offered His guidance and – a fact too often forgotten – exacted complete obedience. He is God, after all. He is the one and only God (Deuteronomy 6:4). And as much as He is love (1 John 4:8) and light (1 John 1:5) and merciful (Deuteronomy 4:31); righteousness and justice are the foundation of His throne (Psalm 89:14); and He values loyalty to Him – and thus His Fatherly instructions – higher than sacrifices (Hosea 6:6).

The content of this book is meant to be read in an attitude of prayer, in the presence of God and in the name of

Jesus Christ, over a leader, for a leader or by a leader. The prayers are written in the form of blessings. Why? Because our God is very partial to blessings and, secondly, curses targeting those in authority abound. Just think what comes out of our mouths sometimes…

These blessings may be directed to God in prayer form for people in authority. Or, if you want to go deeper, you can speak to the respective leaders' spirits directly – there is no distance in the spiritual realm: you are still in the presence of God and covered with the righteousness of His Word (His Son – John 1:14).

Sound foreign? Consider: We are spirit, soul and body. Our spirits are supposed to have dominion (rule over our souls and bodies); there is a hierarchy (1 Thessalonians 5:23). God forms the spirit of man within him (Zechariah 12:1); only a person's spirit understands their thoughts, i.e. which emanate from the soul (1 Corinthians 2:11); it is our spirits that sustain us in sickness (Proverbs 18:14); a crushed spirit does no good (Proverbs 17:22); and we gain our understanding from our spirits (Job 32:8).

Does it not follow that our spirits need nurturing? We are spirit beings and when our lives on earth are over, all that we have left are our spirits and souls. Yet, for the most part, we neglect our spirits and invest a huge amount in our souls and bodies.

One way of nurturing our spirits is by blessing them and acknowledging that they are, in fact, a very valuable part of 'us'.

God started it

Blessing is not a human invention – God started it at creation. He blessed creation (Genesis 1:22); the first thing He did after creating Adam and Eve was to bless them (Genesis 1:28); in Genesis 2:3, God blessed the seventh day – and by extension, all who keep it the way He prescribed; in Genesis 12:2-3, He blessed Abram; in Numbers 6 it is God who blessed the nation. Although that blessing is called the Priestly Blessing, it was only delivered by the priests – God himself blessed the people.

What does all this mean? In English, the word 'bless' has lost much of its potency, and both believers and non-believers bandy it about without realising its value. Hebrew scholars interpret the original Hebrew word for blessing to mean **'to release from restrictions and limitations ... to infuse the object of blessing with unlimited potential and empowerment'**. To bless someone is no small thing!

On the secular front, much research has been done on the effect of positive speech, and the results are rather obvious. I think we can safely say that blessing others or ourselves counts as 'positive speech'. In addition, a great deal of work has been done on the effect of blessing one's spirit. If you want to know more, refer to the decades-long, pioneering work of Arthur Burk of the Sapphire Leadership Group.

In whatever way you want to use these blessings or prayers ('press-ins'?), know that God's Word never returns to

Him void, but always accomplishes that for which He sent it (Isaiah 55:11).

The focus

When I first started out with this book, I wanted to touch on what makes a good leader and what leaders fear most, and then link that to relevant Scriptures. However, the Holy Spirit kept nudging me – my focus was wrong.

It had to start with Him ... with the treasures of wisdom He has laid up for us in His Word and, believe me, this book shares only the tip of the iceberg. All the effects of good and bad leadership can be traced back to either obeying or disobeying God's principles for dealing with people – whether they be nations or the chess team.

It starts with Him. It always has. It always will. All we have to do is to trust His goodness to lead us on secure paths, if we obey.

As you read this book and as you use it to pray over a leader or leadership groups, I want to bless you with probably the most beautiful blessing ever written – by God for His people:

"The Lord bless you-keep you; The Lord make His face shine upon you, and be gracious to you; The Lord lift up His countenance upon you, and give you peace." ' (Numbers 6:24-26)

How to use this book

Let's use 1 Timothy 2:4 as an example from which to craft a prayer/blessing. *"...who desires all men to be saved and to come to the knowledge of the truth."* (NASB)

Prayer

On a point of procedure: We enter His gates with thanksgiving and His courts with praise (Psalm 100:4). After praising God and repenting of any sin that might stand between you and Him, start with, for example, "Father, I bring .... to you, and I pray that You will bless them with the gift of Your salvation. Your Word says that You want all people to be saved and to come to the knowledge and recognition of divine truth ...".

Blessing in prayer

Or, after praising Him, you can start with, "Father, I bring the following leader(s) before your throne. Thank you that Your thoughts toward them are good, to give them a future and a hope (Jeremiah 29:11). I bless .... with Your salvation. I bless .... with coming to the knowledge and recognition of divine truth as Your Word says." Or, after due process, speak to the person directly: ".... I bless you with the gift of salvation. God's Word says that He wants all to be saved and to come to the knowledge and recognition of divine truth. I bless you with accepting this truth".

If you want to pray these blessings over yourself, go for it! It will strengthen your faith (do it out loud, so that you can hear the Word of God) and remind your spirit that God has equipped it for a time such as this.

Chapter 1: Legitimising leadership

Introduction

Leadership is from God. He determines who serves in positions of authority. I am not only referring to authority in the sense of a nation's leadership or a company's leadership. If Sarah, aged 9, has been elected as class president, I believe it was a decision from God – whether her classmates or teachers have a relationship with God or not.

But would He be interested in 'little' leaders? Yes. If the one and only God is interested in the swallow that falls to the ground, if He even knows the number of our hair (Matthew 10:29-31), we can safely accept that He is interested in all of us, all of the time.

Think about the prophet Samuel. According to church historian Josephus, Samuel was about 12 years of age when God spoke to him (actually, to anyone again after a very long silence) for the first time. The Scriptures also clearly refer to "the boy Samuel". And about what did God speak to Samuel? Did He molly-coddle him and talked to him about trivialities like we often do, thinking that children have a junior Holy Spirit? No, His first instruction to the boy Samuel was to share God's judgement of the nation.

And are absolutely all leadership positions filled by God? Yes. Even those of tyrants. Just look at how many times God raised up such leaders purely as a means of disciplining the surrounding nations. (And remember that God can turn the tyrants around too!)

This chapter serves to legitimise the leader. It aims to establish within the leader's spirit the fact that they were chosen by God to fill whatever position they are filling. This is no trivial matter and, inherent, there is the marvellous realisation that, if it was God's decision, surely God's guidance and encouragement can be counted on.

～♫～

Press in

1.

(Leader's name), listen with your spirit to what the Word of God is saying to you. You have been appointed to your position of authority by God, the King of kings. There is no excuse that you can make that will disqualify you from the trust that God has placed in you. Moses made excuses about his speech: God was not daunted. Jeremiah made excuses about his age: God was not daunted. He has established you.

I bless you with the deep realisation that God has sent you and that you do not need to fear what man thinks, or says about you.

> *But the Lord said to me: "Do not say, 'I am a youth.' For you shall go to all to whom I send you, and whatever I command you, you shall speak. Do not be afraid of their faces, for I am with you to deliver you," says the Lord. (Jeremiah 1:7 and 8)*

2.

(Leader), I bless you with the sure knowledge that "not from the east, nor from the west, nor from the desert comes exaltation. But God is the Judge; He puts down one and lifts up another" (Psalm 75:6 and 7).

I bless you with the certainty that David had about his position before God:

So David knew that the Lord had established him as king over Israel, and that He had exalted His kingdom for the sake of His people Israel. (2 Samuel 5:12)

3.

(Leader), I bless you with experiential knowledge that "a man's gift [given in love or courtesy] makes room for him and brings him before great men" (Proverbs 18:16 AMP).

I bless you, (Leader), with godly understanding and knowledge because "when a land does wrong, it has many princes, but when the ruler is a man of understanding and knowledge, its stability endures" (Proverbs 28:2).

May your spirit receive and rejoice in God's picture of what a righteous ruler looks like:

The God of Israel said, The Rock of Israel spoke to me: 'He who rules over men must be just, ruling in the fear of God. And he shall be like the light of the morning without clouds, like the tender grass springing out of the earth, by clear shining after rain.' (2 Samuel 23:3 and 4)

(Leader), I bless you with realising that God placed you on the right learning curriculum before you even knew where you were heading. I bless you with the recognition of your God-ordained skills and experience, and the grace to stand in honour before kings:

> *Do you see a man who excels in his work? He will stand before kings; He will not stand before unknown men. (Proverbs 22:29)*

5.

(Leader), if you have been appointed to a position of authority in an ungodly situation, company or group, I bless you with the encouragement that this is also from God. Be reminded of Daniel who was taken captive to Babylon and through God's intervention, appointed as chief of the magicians. That did not deter Daniel. He remained faithful to his God.

Therefore, I bless you with the revelation – to yourself and to those around you – that the Spirit of the Holy God is in you and that no mystery will trouble you. I bless you that it will also be said of you that illumination, understanding and wisdom are found in you. May an excellent spirit, knowledge and insight be found in you to solve complex problems as the realisation that you were appointed by God sinks in.

> *"Belteshazzar, chief of the magicians, because I know that the Spirit of the Holy God is in you, and no secret troubles you, explain to me the visions of my dream that I have seen, and its interpretation. (Daniel 4:9)*

There is a man in your kingdom in whom is the Spirit of the Holy God. And in the days of your father, light and understanding and wisdom, like the wisdom of the gods, were found in him; and King Nebuchadnezzar your father – your father the king – made him chief of the magicians, astrologers, Chaldeans, and soothsayers. Inasmuch as an excellent spirit, knowledge, understanding, interpreting dreams, solving riddles, and explaining enigmas were found in this Daniel, whom the king named Belteshazzar, now let Daniel be called, and he will give the interpretation. (Daniel 5:11 and 12)

Chapter 2: Knowing God

Introduction

Over and over again, God invites us to know Him. Isn't that absolutely amazing – we serve a God, the only God, who is more powerful than what we could ever imagine and before whom the leadership in heaven is continuously bowing and giving praise (Revelation 4:10,11).

Yet. He wants to be known by us!

This desire of His is not just because He loves us and created us to have close fellowship with Him. Knowing Him unlocks a treasure trove of blessing. It is the compass that keeps us – that keeps leadership – on the right path.

Wilfully not knowing God brings a rebuke:

Your own wickedness will correct you, and your backslidings will rebuke you. Know therefore and see that it is an evil and bitter thing that you have forsaken the Lord your God, and the fear of Me is not in you," says the Lord God of hosts. (Jeremiah 2:19)

If those in authority knew God, not just about Him, but knew and revered Him, our world would be another place altogether. So, now that we have honoured the gift of leadership and the position of the leader as established by God (Chapter 1), we want to bless leaders with knowing God.

Press in

(Leader's name), listen with your spirit to what the Word of God is saying to you. It is in your best interest, as well as in the interest of your constituents, to know God. Knowing God brings depth and authority to you as a leader. It also comforts and encourages you.

We always listen closely to a person's last words. Those whose lives are about to end on earth, generally do not talk frivolously. In their last days or hours, they only share that which has real substance.

Therefore, I would like to bring to your attention the last advice given by King David and Moses (*See 7*).

"As for you, my son Solomon, know the God of your father, and serve Him with a loyal heart and with a willing mind; for the Lord searches all hearts and understands all the intent of the thoughts. If you seek Him, He will be found by you; but if you forsake Him, He will cast you off forever." (1 Chronicles 28:9)

I bless you with a relationship with your heavenly Father that surpasses that of your earthly father. May you have personal knowledge of Him and may your knowledge of Him be ever increasing, just as your love, appreciation and reverence for Him.

May you serve Him with a blameless heart and a willing mind. I bless you with the sensitivity of spirit to know when He is searching your heart and mind, and the alacrity to align your heart and mind with His. Remember that He understands every one of your thoughts – that is reason for both comfort and circumspection.

I bless you with perseverance to seek Him as your vital necessity – because He is! And to discover Him and new facets of Him that He wishes to reveal to you, with joy.

7.

(Leader), I bless you with the ability to clearly hear God's voice and to understand His seasons for your life. I bless you with the authenticity and freedom to be honest with your constituents about the seasons in your life so that they will not be in the dark about major changes about to take place.

I bless you with the right words of encouragement, based on your deep knowledge of God's promises and character for your people in times of change; and the wisdom and generosity to establish and bless your successor in the presence of your constituents.

I bless you with the same encouragement Moses gave his people: *It is the Lord who goes before you; He will be with you. He will not fail you or abandon you. Do not fear or be dismayed.*

Then Moses went and spoke these words to all Israel. And he said to them: "I am one hundred and twenty years old today. I can no longer go out and come in. Also the Lord has said to me, 'You shall not cross over this Jordan.' The Lord your God Himself crosses over before you; He will destroy these nations from before you, and you shall dispossess them. Joshua himself crosses over before you, just as the Lord has said. And the Lord will do to them as He did to Sihon and Og, the kings of the Amorites and their land, when He destroyed them. The Lord will give them over to you, that you may do to them according to every commandment which I have commanded you. Be strong and of good courage, do not fear nor be afraid of them; for the Lord your God, He is the One who goes with you. He will not leave you nor forsake you." Then Moses called Joshua and said to him in the sight of all Israel, "Be strong and of good courage, for you must go with this people to the land which the Lord has sworn to their fathers to give them, and you shall cause them to inherit it. And the Lord, He is the One who goes before you. He will be with you, He will not leave you nor forsake you; do not fear nor be dismayed." (Deuteronomy 31:1-8)

8.

(Leader), I bless you with a keen memory and discernment of God's Word. I bless you with an eagerness to fully surrender your heart to God. Keep always before you not only the fact that He promises to support those who belong to Him, but also the warning that hearts that go astray will have trouble.

For the eyes of the Lord run to and fro throughout the whole earth, to show Himself strong on behalf of those whose heart is loyal to Him. In this you have done foolishly; therefore from now on you shall have wars." (2 Chronicles 16:9)

9.

(Leader), I bless you with a personal spiritual barometer to be able to immediately sense when you are not as close to God as you should be. I bless you to pursue the abundance of God – not only of what He can give, but especially of who He is. May your search and enjoyment of the fountain of living water be your number one priority, so that your own cisterns, meant to quench the thirst of those around you, will always overflow.

Thus says the Lord: What injustice have your fathers found in Me, that they have gone far from Me, have followed idols, and have become idolaters? For My people have committed two evils: They have forsaken Me, the fountain of living waters, and hewn themselves cisterns – broken cisterns that can hold no water. (Jeremiah 2:5 and 13)

10.

(Leader), I bless you with the determination to keep your eyes fixed on God throughout troubled times, to know Him in all things and to give Him the praise due to Him.

I bless you with a humble heart to always realise where you stand in relation to God, and a willing spirit to recognise and appreciate His greatness, His dominion and His Kingship.

I bless you with an understanding of what it means to have reverence for God and the ability to guard your heart against taking offence – God is answerable to no one, but you can know that whatever His will is for your life, it is good.

If you have gone through a period of correction, or if you are to go through such a period in the future (God knows!), I bless you with full restoration and restitution at the God-appointed time, and the right people around you to welcome you back in your rightful place with God.

I bless you with a spirit of praise to exalt the King, and to never be found without proclamations of His goodness and greatness in your heart and mouth.

Pride is like a mist moving under doors and through keyholes. I bless you with an instinctive aversion to pride and haughtiness: may it never be found near you, so that your glory can bring Him glory!

And at the end of the time I, Nebuchadnezzar, lifted my eyes to heaven, and my understanding returned to me; and I blessed the Most High and praised and honored Him who lives forever: For His dominion is an everlasting dominion, and His kingdom is from generation to generation. All the inhabitants of the earth are reputed as nothing; He does according to His will in the army of heaven and among the inhabitants of the earth. No one can restrain His hand or say to Him, "What have You done?" At the same time my reason returned to me, and for the glory of my kingdom, my honor and splendor returned to me. My counselors and nobles resorted to me, I was restored to my kingdom, and excellent majesty was added to me. Now I, Nebuchadnezzar, praise and extol and honor the King of heaven, all of whose works are truth, and His ways justice. And those who walk in pride He is able to put down. (Daniel 4:34-37)

But when his heart was lifted up, and his spirit was hardened in pride, he was deposed from his kingly throne, and they took his glory from him. (Daniel 5:20)

11.

(Leader), you are to honour God first. The best in your storehouse – whether it be finances, time, talents and skills, faithfulness – should be brought to God first. He is not an afterthought. I bless you with the vigilance to honour Him with your best when the entire world seems to be pressuring you into pleasing man first. And I bless you to be aware of God's satisfaction and His grace upon your life for putting Him first.

"You offer defiled food on My altar, but say, 'In what way have we defiled You?' By saying, 'The table of the Lord is contemptible.' And when you offer the blind as a sacrifice, Is it not evil? And when you offer the lame and sick, is it not evil? Offer it then to your governor! Would he be pleased with you? Would he accept you favorably?" Says the Lord of hosts. (Malachi 1:7 and 8)

12.

(Leader), I bless you with the favour of the Lord. I bless you with a desire to know God's ways and the pleasure of being known by Him.

I bless you with the boldness and care to bring those you lead, and in whose lives you have an influence before the Father for His input and blessing.

May you experience His presence in your life and in your decision-making. I bless you with His rest: may you be close enough to Him to easily enter His rest, even in the midst of chaos.

Now therefore, I pray, if I have found grace in Your sight, show me now Your way, that I may know You and that I may find grace in Your sight. And consider that this nation is Your people." And He said, "My Presence will go with you, and I will give you rest." (Exodus 33:13 and 14)

13.

(Leader), in your position, you will have difficulties and successes – wells dug by you that are claimed by others, although you did the work, and wells dug by you that bring forth abundant water and you can claim as yours. I bless you with being close enough to God, and knowing Him well enough to call on His name and acknowledge Him in every circumstance.

So he built an altar there and called on the name of the Lord, and he pitched his tent there; and there Isaac's servants dug a well. (Genesis 26:25)

14.

(Leader), I bless you with not being wise in your own eyes. I bless you to:

Fear the Lord [with reverent awe and obedience] and turn [entirely] away from evil. It will be health to your body [your marrow, your nerves, your sinews, your muscles — all your inner parts] and refreshment (physical well-being) to your bones. Honor the Lord with your wealth and with the first fruits of all your crops (income); then your barns will be abundantly filled and your vats will overflow with new wine. (Proverbs 3:7-10 AMP)

Chapter 3: Righteous leadership

Introduction

God's righteousness is a study on its own. It is one of His qualities that is mentioned most in the Scriptures, but sometimes difficult to grasp. 2 Corinthians 5:21 says that God made Christ, *who knew no sin to be sin for us, that we might become the righteousness of God in Him.*

We are seen as examples of the righteousness of God when we are forgiven – the work which Christ did for us on the cross to reconcile us to God because, without the shedding of blood, there can be no forgiveness of sin (Hebrews 9:22) – and, therefore, in 'right-standing' with God. In speaking about Himself in Luke 4:18, the Salvation of God – Yeshua – quotes Isaiah 61:1-3:

> *"The Spirit of the Lord God is upon Me, because the Lord has anointed Me to preach good tidings to the poor; He has sent Me to heal the broken-hearted, to proclaim liberty to the captives, and the opening of the prison to those who are bound; to proclaim the acceptable year of the Lord, and the day of vengeance of our God; to comfort all who mourn, to console those who mourn in Zion, to give them beauty for ashes, the oil of joy for mourning, the garment of praise for the spirit of heaviness; that they may be called trees of righteousness, the planting of the Lord, that He may be glorified."*

Abram – who lived ages before the Word was made flesh among men (John 1:14), ... *believed in the Lord, and He accounted it to him for righteousness.* (Genesis 15:6). Righteousness in leadership is non-negotiable.

～❦～

Press in

15.

(Leader), I bless you with the ability to judge righteously in every circumstance. I bless you with seeing from God's perspective – in perfect truth – so that you are not swayed by the outward appearances of man.

> *You shall do no injustice in judgment. You shall not be partial to the poor, nor honor the person of the mighty. In righteousness you shall judge your neighbor. (Leviticus 19:15)*

16.

(Leader), know and understand that the Lord will recompense you according to your righteousness. Therefore, I bless you with fervour to remain in right-standing with God; to not let your guard down for one moment through compromise, which takes your eyes off Him and leads to sin.

> *Therefore the Lord has recompensed me according to my righteousness, according to my cleanness in His eyes. (2 Samuel 22:25)*

17.

(Leader), I bless you with the realisation that God delighted in positioning you for leadership. Know and understand that He has put you in that position to perform with justice and righteousness. Celebrate the fact that He will guide you in all righteousness, if you will surrender to Him and know Him in all your ways.

Blessed be the Lord your God, who delighted in you, setting you on His throne to be king for the Lord your God! Because your God has loved Israel, to establish them forever, therefore He made you king over them, to do justice and righteousness. (2 Chronicles 9:8)

18.

(Leader), God is righteous. There is absolutely no room in His being and His Kingdom for unrighteousness – He cannot look upon it. When He turns His head away, in a manner of speaking, our spiritual enemy and natural enemies have a field day. I bless you with being righteous, in right-standing with God, in all your dealings.

I bless you with being resolute in paying fair wages and conducting business, or ruling fairly. I bless you with being aware of the needs of others and to intervene in those needs by using the gifts – whether skills-based or financial – God has given you to address those needs, to defend the afflicted and needy, and not to turn a blind eye.

I bless you with a fresh revelation of God's value of righteousness, a willing spirit to comply, and sensitivity to His joy at you walking with Him in righteousness and knowing Him.

"Woe to him who builds his house by unrighteousness and his chambers by injustice, Who uses his neighbor's service without wages and gives him nothing for his work, Who says, 'I will build myself a wide house with spacious chambers, and cut out windows for it, paneling it with cedar and painting it with vermilion.' "Shall you reign because you enclose yourself in cedar? Did not your father eat and drink, and do justice and righteousness? Then it was well with him. He judged the cause of the poor and needy; then it was well. Was not this knowing Me?" says the Lord. (Jeremiah 22:13-16)

Chapter 4: Wisdom

Introduction

It is worthwhile to focus on what God's Word says about wisdom – treat yourself to a Word study on the topic. It would seem that God does not place a particularly high value on our human wisdom, so best we pursue His!

One of the best examples of wisdom given to a leader is that of Solomon. His story is both encouraging and tragic. His rule was characterised by wisdom and the kingdom flourished in material aspects, as well as in peace. However, he disregarded God's fatherly instruction that no other god besides Him should be worshipped. As his wives multiplied, so did the number of gods he had to appease. 1 Kings 11:4 says, *For it was so, when Solomon was old, that his wives turned his heart after other gods; and his heart was not loyal to the Lord his God, as was the heart of his father David.*

It is particularly interesting to see that God refers to Wisdom as a person, not an obscure concept. Over and over, we read in the Scriptures that Wisdom calls, she stands on the path – Wisdom is waiting to respond to those who want to partner with her.

Many people confuse wisdom with common sense. Sometimes, because the person already has a relationship with Wisdom, their common sense is sufficiently astute to pass for wisdom. However, it would seem that, for the majority, the truth about common sense is that it is, in fact, not so common…

If we lack wisdom, He invites us in James 1:5 to ... *ask of God, who gives to all liberally and without reproach, and it will be given to him.*

Luke 7:35 says that *wisdom is justified by all her children.*

Isn't that just so true? It is very easy to differentiate the wise from the foolish – just look at the fruit of their words and actions.

The apostle Paul prayed *That the God of our Lord Jesus Christ, the Father of glory, may give to you the spirit of wisdom and revelation in the knowledge of Him* (Ephesians 1:17). May that be our prayer for ourselves too – and for our leaders.

⌁

Press in

19.

(Leader), listen with your spirit to the Word of God for you. I bless you with ears attentive to godly wisdom and a heart that eagerly seeks out wisdom. I bless you with the boldness to cry out for insight and understanding, and not to be intimidated by those around you who think that your position of authority means that you already have wisdom in tow.

I bless you with the desire to seek the wisdom that comes from God as you would seek a treasure. In your seeking, you will find it – God promises, and you will understand the reverent fear of God. May the knowing of just how awesome (awe-inspiring, breath-taking, fearsome, overwhelming) He is permeate your very being. May your appetite for knowing God increase daily.

I bless you, as you exponentially grow in wisdom, to get to know God as your shield because you walk in integrity. He guards the paths of justice and He preserves your way – may you be intently aware of His faithfulness in every good path.

Listen:

So that you incline your ear to wisdom, and apply your heart to understanding; Yes, if you cry out for discernment, and lift up your voice for understanding, If you seek her as silver, and search for her as for hidden treasures; Then you will understand the fear of the Lord, and find the knowledge of God. For the Lord gives wisdom; from His mouth come knowledge and understanding; He stores up sound wisdom for the upright; He is a shield to those who walk uprightly; He guards the paths of justice, and preserves the way of His saints. Then you will understand righteousness and justice, equity and every good path. (Proverbs 2:2-9)

20.

(Leader), the Word of God is replete with calls for us to increase in wisdom. So, again, I bless you to increase in godly wisdom; let it be your pre-eminent desire. Wisdom will honour you, if you embrace her.

Then, (Leader), I bless you with believing and accepting that God is a God whose Word is true – if He promised something, He will do it! Accept that He has heard your petition and that He has granted your request for wisdom. He has instructed you in the way of godly wisdom and He has led you in upright paths. Trust that when you walk in obedience, your steps will be sure and safe. I bless you with faith to overcome any insecurity you might have where wise decision-making is concerned. Believe Him!

> *Wisdom is the principal thing; therefore get wisdom. And in all your getting, get understanding. Exalt her, and she will promote you; she will bring you honor, when you embrace her. I have taught you in the way of wisdom; I have led you in the right paths. When you walk, your steps will not be hindered, and when you run, you will not stumble. (Proverbs 4:7, 8, 11 and 12)*

21.

(Leader), I bless you with discernment to see Wisdom when she beckons to you. The Word says she takes her stand where the paths meet – where you have to make a decision altering the course of business or someone else's course. She waits at the entrance of a door – there where you have to enter to either another business opportunity, or a sphere of influence. She waits to be called on by you: Hear her calling!

I bless you, (Leader), to be open-minded and humble enough to recognise that you need wisdom and to then seek that astute insight; to understand what you receive and to value this free gift that leads to godly living above earthly treasure.

> *She takes her stand on the top of the high hill, beside the way, where the paths meet. She cries out by the gates, at the entry of the city, at the entrance of the doors: "To you, O men, I call, and my voice is to the sons of men. O you simple ones, understand prudence, and you fools, be of an understanding heart. (Proverbs 8:2-5)*

22.

(Leader), hear again and let it settle deep within your spirit: no earthy treasure can compare with wisdom. It is, truly, the gift that keeps on giving. I bless you with revelling in the gifts that come with wisdom, should you seek them. Good judgement, moral courage, knowledge and discretion are yours, if you embrace wisdom. I bless you with the capacity and hunger for all of these things.

I bless you with a reverent fear of God and with having a relationship where you hate what He hates: evil, pride and arrogance, and a perverted mouth. Do the maths, (Leader): the fear of the Lord is the beginning of wisdom. The fear of the Lord is to hate evil. Therefore, to hate evil is the beginning of wisdom.

I bless you with such conviction in the presence of evil – in whatever shape or form it might present itself in your sphere of influence – that you will shun it outright. I bless you with counsel from the throne room of God, with understanding, power and strength.

I bless you with the sure knowledge that you reign and rule, decide and decree justice because of God. I bless you to govern rightly.

I bless you to know the love of God, and with the physical and spiritual fortitude to seek Him early, in the midst of a busy schedule. Then you will find Him. I bless you to enjoy His riches and honour, His enduring wealth and righteousness.

For wisdom is better than rubies, and all the things one may desire cannot be compared with her. "I, wisdom, dwell with prudence, and find out knowledge and discretion. The fear of the Lord is to hate evil;

pride and arrogance and the evil way and the perverse mouth I hate. Counsel is mine, and sound wisdom; I am understanding, I have strength. By me kings reign, and rulers decree justice. By me princes rule, and nobles, all the judges of the earth. I love those who love me, and those who seek me diligently will find me. Riches and honor are with me, enduring riches and righteousness. (Proverbs 8:11-18)

"The fear of the Lord is the beginning of wisdom, and the knowledge of the Holy One is understanding. (Proverbs 9:10)

23.

(Leader), I bless you with remembering that the reverent fear and worship of the Lord is the beginning of wisdom and skill. I bless you with knowing wisdom in your inmost heart. May your rule or tenure be characterised by understanding, wisdom and meaning.

And to man He said, 'Behold, the fear of the Lord, that is wisdom, and to depart from evil is understanding.' (Job 28:28)

Behold, You desire truth in the inward parts, and in the hidden part You will make me to know wisdom. (Psalm 51:6)

The fear of the Lord is the beginning of wisdom; a good understanding have all those who do His commandments. His praise endures forever. (Psalm 111:10)

24.

(Leader), I bless you with the ability to get to know Wisdom as the Master Craftsman. Wisdom was with the Father when, in shaking, the heavens and the earth were created. Wisdom is with you as you walk out your destiny; as the God-breath in you continues to create even now. May you experience Wisdom as God's delight; may you – because you share in that Wisdom in a profound way – rejoice before the living God always.

Then I was beside Him as a master craftsman; and I was daily His delight, rejoicing always before Him, (Proverbs 8:30)

25.

(Leader), as you enquire after Wisdom and as you pay attention to Wisdom, know that you are also happy, prosperous and to be admired. You are blessed! Be blessed to know that you have found life; you have obtained favour and grace with God.

Hear instruction and be wise, and do not disdain it. Blessed is the man who listens to me, watching daily at my gates, waiting at the posts of my doors. For whoever finds me finds life, and obtains favor from the Lord. (Proverbs 8:33-35)

26.

(Leader), I bless you with preserving your own soul because you have gained wisdom and good sense. I bless you with finding good and with prospering because you keep understanding. I bless you to listen to counsel, to receive instruction and accept correction, so that you will be wise in the time to come.

He who gets wisdom loves his own soul; he who keeps understanding will find good. Listen to counsel and receive instruction, that you may be wise in your latter days. (Proverbs 19:8 and 20)

27.

(Leader), I bless you with a wise tongue to speak knowledge that is pleasing and acceptable. Reject the way of the fool. Let Wisdom make her home in your heart and mind, and allow your mouth to overflow with that [wisdom] which fills your heart.

The tongue of the wise uses knowledge rightly, but the mouth of fools pours forth foolishness. (Proverbs 15:2)

28.

(Leader), we can learn a number of lessons from the account of Isaac opening the wells of his father and experiencing opposition. Firstly, I bless you with the wisdom to identify those things of value established or implemented by your predecessors. It is true that, through you, God might want to establish a new thing or herald a new season and I bless you with the wisdom to hear from Him what that new thing is. However, He is outside of time and His principles stand from everlasting to everlasting.

I bless you with the wisdom to enquire of Him what He wants to re-open: which channels that might have been forgotten He wants to use for blessing. And then I bless you with the strength of character to openly honour the predecessor on whose foundation you are building your success.

And Isaac dug again the wells of water which they had dug in the days of Abraham his father, for the Philistines had stopped them up after the death of Abraham. He called them by the names which his father had called them. (Genesis 26:18)

(Leader), I bless you with the ability and wisdom to select your battles – whether in your personal life, in the boardroom or on the world stage. Isaac opened more than one of his father's wells and, each time, the opposition was such that the benefits of fighting for the wells could not outweigh the damages.

I bless you with the wisdom to know when to stop fighting. God could have intervened in Isaac's situation at any time – one word could have sent the enemy running. But God had another plan. He had another piece of land in mind for Isaac, where He wanted Isaac to settle for that season. I bless you with the wisdom to recognise when God has something else for you to take possession of. I bless you with the wisdom to recognise God's seasons in your life.

I bless you with the room that God has for you and with the prosperity that He has in store for you as you boldly, in wisdom and obedience, walk away from a fight that is not yours to fight anymore.

> *Also Isaac's servants dug in the valley, and found a well of running water there. But the herdsmen of Gerar quarreled with Isaac's herdsmen, saying, "The water is ours." So he called the name of the well Esek, because they quarreled with him. Then they dug another well, and they quarreled over that one also. So he called its name Sitnah. And he moved from there and dug another well, and they did not quarrel over it. So he called its name Rehoboth, because he said, "For now the Lord has made room for us, and we shall be fruitful in the land." (Genesis 26:19-22)*

(Leader), there is great wisdom in humility. I bless you with humility. I bless you with a right understanding of what it means to be humble and with the courage to favour humility over pride.

In your life, you have had, and will have, trials and uphill battles. I bless you with the strength of spirit to endure, but also with the gentleness of spirit to remain flexible and teachable as you walk humbly with God. Let your successes be lifted up to God in thanksgiving and praise. Let your failures be lifted up to Him as necessary sacrifices and opportunities to learn, grow and obtain more wisdom.

I bless you to share God's aversion to false balances and dishonest business practices. Be offended by it because He is offended by it. I bless you to delight in accurate scales, and in righteous and fair business practices. Pride leads to shame and dishonour.

I bless you to be vigilant and to guard against arrogance or self-importance. I bless you with the wisdom to both reject such thoughts and feelings, and to flee from those who through vain flattery seek to establish such in your heart. Be wise!

Dishonest scales are an abomination to the Lord, but a just weight is His delight. When pride comes, then comes shame; but with the humble is wisdom. (Proverbs 11:1 and 2)

31.

(Leader), think of your position and your sphere of influence as a house. I bless you and pray that Wisdom will build the house that the Father has entrusted to you. By understanding, it will be established on a good foundation. I bless every facet of that house. By the knowledge offered by Wisdom, every unit, department, employee and constituent will be filled with precious and pleasant riches.

Through wisdom a house is built, and by understanding it is established; by knowledge the rooms are filled with all precious and pleasant riches. (Proverbs 24:3 and 4)

32.

(Leader), I bless you to pay attention to the Word of God and to find good. I bless you with trusting God. May you have a cognitive and deeply spiritual understanding of how blessed you are because you trust in the Lord. I bless you to recognise and know that Wisdom is in your life and that, therefore, you have a future and a reward. I bless you with surety that your hope and expectation shall not be cut off because you have sought after Wisdom, have paid attention to Wisdom and treasure God's Wisdom above all other treasures.

He who heeds the word wisely will find good, and whoever trusts in the Lord, happy is he. (Proverbs 16:20)

So shall the knowledge of wisdom be to your soul; if you have found it, there is a prospect, and your hope will not be cut off. (Proverbs 24:14)

33.

(Leader), wisdom is as good as an inheritance. I bless you with this realisation, and with the joy of possessing and having free access to something so precious. I bless you with the protection offered by wisdom: it shields and preserves your life. I bless you with the realisation that while both wisdom and money are defences, it is only wisdom that has the promise that it gives life to those who have it.

Wisdom is good with an inheritance, and profitable to those who see the sun. For wisdom is a defense as money is a defense, but the excellence of knowledge is that wisdom gives life to those who have it. (Ecclesiastes 7:11 and 12)

34.

(Leader), I bless you with an understanding mind and a hearing heart with which to lead your people. I bless you with the ability to justly discern between good and evil. God knows the way you should go. He knows you by name and every single person in your care.

There is none more qualified to lead, judge and care for those over whom you have been appointed than Him. Be wise and not only recognise and acknowledge this, but also draw strength from it. Make Him a part of your decision-making in every way and you will reap an abundant harvest.

Therefore give to Your servant an understanding heart to judge Your people, that I may discern between good and evil. For who is able to judge this great people of Yours? (1 Kings 3:9)

Chapter 5: Stewardship

Introduction

Synonyms for 'stewardship' include *care, control, maintenance, management, protection, supervision, attention, governing, guardianship* and *custody.* Stewardship is high on God's agenda – right up there with procreation, actually. It was one of the first things He said to Adam and Eve after He blessed them: *Then God blessed them, and God said to them, "Be fruitful and multiply; fill the earth and subdue it; have dominion over the fish of the sea, over the birds of the air, and over every living thing that moves on the earth."* (Genesis 1:28)

Contrary to popular belief, the oldest profession is that of leadership, in particular, stewardship of the earth and every living creature on the earth.

That instruction was not negated when Adam and Eve handed their authority over the earth to Satan. It just became harder. Leadership – and stewardship – is hard because of our sinful nature, because of our motives that are continually centred on self-preservation and 'getting ahead'.

Matthew 25:14-30 relates the parable of a wealthy man going on a trip and entrusting a certain amount of money to three of his servants. Upon returning, he required a reckoning of how the servants had stewarded his money. The first two did well, having doubled what he gave them. The third acted foolishly (by not doing the sensible thing to at least deposit the money in the bank and earn interest), demonstrated his laziness (by not using his skills, for which he had been employed to increase his master's money), and advanced an excuse infused with fear (hiding the money and using the master's demanding nature as an excuse for not trying). That servant lost the little that he had.

God is serious about good stewardship and we have to pray for our leaders to steward what has been entrusted to them responsibly and righteously.

~⁓~

Press in

(Leader), listen with your spirit to what the Spirit of God is saying to you through His Word. Be diligent to know the condition of that which has been placed in your care. While you might have competent people under you to help share the burden, the ultimate responsibility lies with you. God will require an account from you. I bless you with being present. I bless you with having the determination to have your finger on the pulse of your company or nation.

I bless you with courage to face whatever challenge might arise and not to bury your head in the sand, thinking someone else will meet the challenge. Seasons change. It might go well now, or it might be a difficult time, but it is only by being present and knowing the condition of your flocks that you can plan for your household.

Be diligent to know the state of your flocks, and attend to your herds; for riches are not forever, nor does a crown endure to all generations. When the hay is removed, and the tender grass shows itself, and the herbs of the mountains are gathered in, the lambs will provide your clothing, and the goats the price of a field; You shall have enough goats' milk for your food, for the food of your household, and the nourishment of your maidservants. (Proverbs 27:23-27)

36.

(Leader), I bless you with doing what you know has to be done. In times where you have no idea what is coming, or how to proceed, do what you know to do. When God established His everlasting covenant with Abram, God did everything. Abram did not play any role except to do what God asked him to do and listen to the promise. He brought the animals, cut them in half and placed the pieces in two parallel rows. God did not give any other instruction. The birds of prey came down and Abram did what he knew to do – he stewarded (guarded, looked after) the imminent sign of the covenant – and drove the birds away. That's all, so simple. I bless you, (Leader), with peace to do what you know to do until such time as God reveals the next step.

And when the vultures came down on the carcasses, Abram drove them away. (Genesis 15:11)

37.

(Leader), firstly, I bless you with the ability and integrity to steward your appetite for wealth and power. Abram had a legitimate right to take the king of Sodom up on his offer to keep the spoil after the battle to save the captured Lot. He was not greedy, however, and he understood the ramifications of taking the spoil. I bless you, secondly, with the insight to rightly judge the implications to your reputation in every circumstance and decision. Thirdly, I bless you to look after your people, even if you gain nothing. All too often, a leader's sense of entitlement makes them lose sight of their people's needs. Abram stewarded his people: he made sure they had enough to eat and that they received their part of the booty as payment for fighting on his behalf. I bless you with doing right by your people.

> *But Abram said to the king of Sodom, "I have raised my hand to the Lord, God Most High, the Possessor of heaven and earth, that I will take nothing, from a thread to a sandal strap, and that I will not take anything that is yours, lest you should say, 'I have made Abram rich'— except only what the young men have eaten, and the portion of the men who went with me: Aner, Eshcol, and Mamre; let them take their portion." (Genesis 14:22-24)*

38.

(Leader), I bless you with the presence of mind and courage to bring justice to pass speedily. Justice and ensuring fair dealings are part and parcel of stewardship. I bless you with following the example set by God. Aaron and Miriam talked against Moses because of the wife he took – seemingly a small thing: they gossiped and criticised their brother for his choice in women. God did not wait for a disciplinary; He did not establish a committee to meet about the issue; He did not wait to see what would happen next, whether they would self-correct. Instead, the Word says that "suddenly" He spoke to them – all three of them – and called them aside.

At the very moment that His servant, and the one with whom He spoke face-to-face, was being dishonoured, He exercised discipline. I bless you, (Leader), to execute your sentences of judgement quickly. If you do not, the Word says, "the hearts of the sons of men are fully set to do evil" and when that situation persists, Habakkuk 1:4 says, *"...the law is ineffective and ignored and justice is never upheld, for the wicked surround the righteous; therefore, justice becomes perverted"*. Do not allow evil to get a foothold – no matter how insignificant it might look – be diligent, be just!

> *Suddenly the Lord said to Moses, Aaron, and Miriam, "Come out, you three, to the tabernacle of meeting!" So the three came out. Then the Lord came down in the pillar of cloud and stood in the door of the tabernacle, and called Aaron and Miriam. And they both went forward. (Numbers 12:4 and 5)*

> *Because the sentence against an evil work is not executed speedily, therefore the heart of the sons of men is fully set in them to do evil. (Ecclesiastes 8:11)*

39.

(Leader), I bless you with taking your role as steward seriously. Your responsibility towards those around you is greater than what is expected from others because you have the platform and authority to influence people's choices. I bless you with not turning a blind eye to the destructive behaviour of those in your care.

I bless you with wisdom and love to "rescue those who are being taken away to death and those who stagger to the slaughter". Claiming ignorance will not stand before God. I bless you with willingness to ask God how you should address destructive behaviour within the remit of country or company regulations, so that you may act with wisdom. I bless you with open ears and an obedient heart to follow God's instructions. I bless you with favour from the Father, so that, when He judges you according to your works in this matter, you will not be found lacking, but you will experience His pleasure at having conducted yourself as a good and faithful steward.

Deliver those who are drawn toward death, and hold back those stumbling to the slaughter. If you say, "Surely we did not know this," does not He who weighs the hearts consider it? He who keeps your soul, does He not know it? And will He not render to each man according to his deeds? (Proverbs 24:11 and 12)

40.

(Leader), I bless you with a right attitude and a servant heart. I bless you to help those who need help and to restore that which needs restoring, if it is in your power to do so. And to do so immediately. I bless you with stewarding those in your charge with compassion, and with honouring their dignity.

Do not withhold good from those to whom it is due, when it is in the power of your hand to do so. Do not say to your neighbor, "Go, and come back, and tomorrow I will give it," when you have it with you. (Proverbs 3:27 and 28)

Chapter 6: Behaviour

Introduction

Nothing says 'leader' or 'follower' or even 'fool' like the way we behave and speak.

The Word of God is, from start to finish, a romance of God's faithful pursuit of His wayward creation, as well as a manual for godly behaviour. It was not given because He is a spoil sport or just really, really uppity. He instructs us on how to behave in every facet of life because the fall in the Garden of Eden decimated any close and authentic relationship we might have had with the living God. We lost our ability to behave in a way worthy of our potential – the potential inherent in us as being created in His image. Much of our behaviour is linked to self-interest or control (a symptom of fear).

Our behaviour is determined by how close our connection is with Him. And He wants to connect very closely with each and every person on earth – that is why He created us. If He wanted someone to boss around, He would have made robots with shiny heads and vocabularies limited to "Yes, Sir".

We can try and behave 'correctly', but that either does not last very long, or it is founded on suffocating legalism. The only time that we seem to be able to consciously change our behaviour is when there is already a close relationship with God.

You see, when we love Him with all our heart, and mind and strength, as He asks, we want to please Him and then change comes more easily. Sometimes, we are not really aware of the change – but as we are transformed in His image, certain adjustments take place without us even realising it. Relationship comes first, then obedience.

When we pray for leaders to change their behaviour, God can, of course, cause that to happen without the leader having any relationship with Him (He holds the heart of the king in His hand, after all [Proverbs 21:1]). He can sovereignly change a leader's behaviour.

But, I believe that is not His first choice. His first choice is that the leader comes to repentance, comes to know God in His fullness and accepts His invitation to have a Father-son relationship.

So, as we pray for leaders' behaviour to come in line with God's heart and Word, let's also pray for the reconciliation of the leader with God. It will also change our hearts, as we would be less inclined to pray with judgement.

Allow God to show you His heart for the particular leader – you will be surprised and blessed, and will pray with a new fervour and insight.

These following prayers cover broad behavioural topics such as humility, mercy and kindness, gracious speech and integrity. There are hundreds more in the Scriptures – look for them and craft your own blessing for those in authority.

knows Me, that I am the Lord, exercising lovingkindness, judgment,
and righteousness in the earth. For in these I delight," says the Lord.
(Jeremiah 9:23-24)

44.

(Leader), in your tenure, there will be people who support you, and there will be others who regard you with contempt and seek to undermine you. I bless you with a heart that is right before God, so that your behaviour towards both these groups will bring Him honour – and, in turn, He will honour you. I bless you not to rise to the bait of those seeking to humiliate you.

I bless you with a forgiving heart attitude. If you follow after God in righteousness and humility, He will vindicate you in the right season. When that happens, I bless you to remain in the right attitude and not give way to revenge. I bless you to rise above what human nature might dictate and to keep your eyes fixed on God – seeing Him in this situation and remembering what He has done for you.

I bless you with alacrity of spirit to acknowledge Him, thereby making room for mercy towards those who foolishly seek to undermine your authority.

And Saul also went home to Gibeah; and valiant men went with him,
whose hearts God had touched. But some rebels said, "How can this
man save us?" So they despised him, and brought him no presents.
But he held his peace. (1 Samuel 10:26-27)

Then the people said to Samuel, "Who is he who said, 'Shall Saul
reign over us?' Bring the men, that we may put them to death." But

Saul said, "Not a man shall be put to death this day, for today the Lord has accomplished salvation in Israel." (1 Samuel 11:12-13)

45.

(Leader), I bless you with realising that what God asks of you is not difficult; it is not unreasonable. I bless you with being just and loving, and practising kindness, and walking humbly with God. I bless you with setting aside any inflated sense of self-importance and self-righteousness. Then it will go well with you.

He has shown you, O man, what is good; and what does the Lord require of you but to do justly, to love mercy, and to walk humbly with your God? (Micah 6:8)

46.

(Leader), I bless you with finding favour and esteem in the sight of God and man. I bless you with adhering to the principles of God that lead to such favour. I bless you to be known for your mercy, kindness and truth. In whichever circles you might move, in whatever decisions you have to make, let mercy, kindness and truth be your guide. I bless you to let these qualities – together with godly wisdom and righteousness – become such a part of your leadership style and behaviour that they might as well be written on your heart.

And, (Leader), if you have not known any of these qualities, if you have been treated with cruelty and deceit, I bless you with the ability to forgive those who have treated you this way. I ask the Father of forgiveness and mercy to help you overcome the pain and trauma of the behaviour of others.

I bless you with His forgiveness and healing. I bless you with finding comfort and peace in being merciful, kind and truthful. I bless you, again, to taste with delight His favour and esteem of you.

Let not mercy and truth forsake you; bind them around your neck, write them on the tablet of your heart, and so find favor and high esteem in the sight of God and man. (Proverbs 3:3-4)

47.

(Leader), I bless you with kindness that leads to expression, to action. I bless you with eyes that see and a heart and hand that respond to need. I bless you to generously give to those who have need. If you find the reality of the number of people in need too daunting or overwhelming, I bless you with not taking the easy way out and adopting an ostrich mentality.

I bless you with being honest before the Lord about your perceptions, feelings and doubts, so that He can show you where He wants you to give. Trust Him to know best. I bless you with the sheer delight of giving freely to others because you have received so much.

I bless you with experiencing the smile of the Father as you are His hands and feet on earth, mending what is broken. I bless you with pleasing the sovereign God, the One that no-one can out-give. I bless you with receiving your just reward for giving to those in need with a cheerful heart.

He who has pity on the poor lends to the Lord, and He will pay back what he has given. (Proverbs 19:17)

48.

(Leader), I bless you with the necessary mind shift to accept that, more than anything else, your position is upheld by loving-kindness. I bless you with making kindness one of the pillars of your leadership style and behaviour. It is not a show of power or posturing that will help you in the day you need protection: that is the response of broken people.

I bless you with rising in your position of authority and letting that which baffles the seemingly wise, be your guiding principles. I bless you with being protected by loyalty and mercy, truth and faithfulness, as the Word of God promises.

Mercy and truth preserve the king, and by lovingkindness he upholds his throne. (Proverbs 20:28)

49.

(Leader), the human heart is wicked and given to all sorts of responses displeasing to God. When justice is done, we often do not rejoice in justice, but rather in that the perpetrator got his just deserts. I bless you with responding in the opposite spirit. I bless you with rising above the feeling of gladness when your enemy falls. I bless you with being thankful to God for fighting on your behalf.

I bless you to be sensitive to the motivations of your heart: there is a big difference between thanking God for His intervention and rejoicing in your opponent's stumbling. I bless you with understanding that delighting in your opponent's changed fate by, for example, mocking him, will make you, in

God's eyes, a worse offender and you will reap the consequences of your behaviour. I also bless you with kindness not to kick your opponent while he is down. Obadiah admonishes not to loot treasures in the day of his ruin.

Do not rejoice when your enemy falls, and do not let your heart be glad when he stumbles; lest the Lord see it, and it displease Him, and He turn away His wrath from him. (Proverbs 24:17 and 18)

"But you should not have gazed on the day of your brother in the day of his captivity; nor should you have rejoiced over the children of Judah in the day of their destruction; nor should you have spoken proudly in the day of distress. You should not have entered the gate of My people in the day of their calamity. Indeed, you should not have gazed on their affliction in the day of their calamity, nor laid hands on their substance in the day of their calamity. (Obadiah 12 and 13)

50.

(Leader), I bless you with reverential boldness before God. This is not incongruous. Both Moses and Abram (and King David, and …) had the highest respect and reverence for God, but they also had a boldness to question God and to defend, or ask for mercy for those in their care. The wonder of this is that God allows it! I bless you with such a relationship with God – He wants to commune with you and that means that you have freedom to speak your mind: He can handle it!

I bless you with your kindness and mercy towards others making room for you to ask God for pardon on their behalf. Abram reverentially pushed the boundaries when he interceded for Sodom and Gomorrah before the Lord. I bless you, (Leader), with a merciful and kind heart to boldly draw close to God's throne of grace.

Abraham's petition stopped at 10 righteous because the custom and culture of the time determined that a meeting of 10 righteous people was the smallest number denoting a government. I bless you with learning and understanding what constitutes a quorum before God to influence the destiny of the bigger group. May God surround you with sufficient righteous people to help you steward the responsibility of Godly leadership.

> *So the Lord said, If I find in Sodom fifty righteous within the city, then I will spare all the place for their sakes. Then Abraham answered and said, "Indeed now, I who am but dust and ashes have taken it upon myself to speak to the Lord: 'Suppose there were five less than the fifty righteous; would You destroy all the city for lack of five? So He said, "If I find there forty-five, I will not destroy it." Then he said, "Let not the Lord be angry, and I will speak but once more. Suppose ten should be found there? And He said, I will not destroy it for the sake of ten. (Genesis 18:26-28 and 32)*

51.

(Leader), I bless you with guarding your heart and being mindful of what you allow to come out of your mouth. I bless you with a holy tongue and with your whole being recognising and giving the honour due to God. I bless you with an obedient heart. Be obedient to His instruction that His name is not to be taken in vain. I bless you with a revelation of the power behind His name and to treat it with reverence.

I bless you with a reverential fear for His name, but also with the comfort, peace, victory and thousands of other benefits contained within His name.

You shall not take the name of the Lord your God in vain, for the Lord will not hold him guiltless who takes His name in vain. (Exodus 20:7)

52.

(Leader), I bless you with liberation from any form of conceit. I bless you with the mettle to take stock of who you are and where you are. I bless you with grasping the kindness of God that you do not have to stay where you are! Be free in His presence to ask for a pure heart and clean lips – He is only too ready to grant your request.

I bless you with having your lips touched and purified by a live coal from the altar. Rejoice that your iniquity and guilt have been taken away, and that your sin is forgiven.

Isaiah was only released in his calling after his iniquity was removed (verses 8 and 9). I bless you with pursuing a clean slate before the Lord, where your generational iniquities are also cleansed so that God can release you to reach your maximum potential and bring Him honour in this life.

So I said: "Woe is me, for I am undone! Because I am a man of unclean lips, and I dwell in the midst of a people of unclean lips; for my eyes have seen the King, the Lord of hosts." Then one of the seraphim flew to me, having in his hand a live coal which he had taken with the tongs from the altar. And he touched my mouth with it, and said: "Behold, this has touched your lips; your iniquity is taken away, and your sin purged." (Isaiah 6:5-7)

53.

(Leader), again I bless you with watching over your heart. From your heart – your centre, where you have your deepest thoughts, convictions, motivations – flows the springs of life. I bless you with a pure heart from which truth will flow. I bless you that the fruit of your mouth will be truth. I bless you with sincerity that expels and overrides any form of lying, deceit and dishonesty.

Keep your heart with all diligence, for out of it spring the issues of life. Put away from you a deceitful mouth, and put perverse lips far from you. (Proverbs 4:23 and 24)

54.

(Leader), make no mistake: Your tongue is a powerful organ. James 3:4 and 5 likens the tongue to a rudder that steers big ships through rough winds wherever the helmsman decides.

I bless you, (Leader), with understanding that death and life are in the power of the tongue. May that thought grip your heart; may it cause you to cultivate words that are life-giving, words that establish those in your care on their respective growth paths.

I bless you with an abundance of good fruit from your lips and with the enjoyment of reaping good consequences from your words. I bless you with wisdom not to indulge in speaking, if your words are not pure, uplifting and the truth spoken in love – for you will eat that fruit as well.

Death and life are in the power of the tongue, and those who love it will eat its fruit. (Proverbs 18:21)

55.

(Leader), I bless you with a pure heart and gracious speech. I bless you with a deep understanding of the exquisite value attached to these qualities. God's Word says that you will have the king as your friend. Your pure heart and gracious speech will cause you to stand before those in high authority. Not only that, but you will have the King of kings as your friend. I bless you with a desire to have that kind of relationship with God. I bless you with a heart and speech that are overflowing with that which brings excellence to life, which allows those in your care to shine and reach their potential, bringing great honour to the King.

He who loves purity of heart and has grace on his lips, the king will be his friend. (Proverbs 22:11)

56.

(Leader), I bless you with sensitivity to the Holy Spirit and a willingness to yield to the Spirit's direction. I bless you with faith and trust that the Spirit will show you what to speak at the right time. I bless you with experiencing that, when your thoughts and speech are guided by God, your words will be like apples of gold in settings of silver – they will be beautiful and precious; people will want to hear them. I bless you not only with the right words, but also with wisdom to determine to speak at the right time and place, so that you are in complete alignment with God and His purposes for you in any situation or forum.

A word fitly spoken is like apples of gold in settings of silver. (Proverbs 25:11)

57.

(Leader), I bless you with discernment when a flatterer or liar crosses your path. Do not be deceived, they wish you – and by extension, those in your care – harm. Do not lend your ears to a lying tongue and do not, yourself, use your tongue for such purposes. Do not trust the flatterer, and you yourself, do not engage in flattery where the purpose is to manipulate or distract. I bless you with wisdom and a ready response when these people seek to work ruin by their behaviour.

A lying tongue hates those who are crushed by it, and a flattering mouth works ruin. (Proverbs 26:28)

58.

(Leader), I bless you with the anointing that rested on Levi when true instruction – teaching, coaching, commanding – and justice came from his mouth. I bless you with a firm foundation for such an anointing in your life; that you would walk in peace and uprightness with God. I bless your words with the necessary authority to turn many away from wickedness.

The law of truth was in his mouth, and injustice was not found on his lips. He walked with Me in peace and equity, and turned many away from iniquity. (Malachi 2:6)

(Leader), I bless you with a good name. I bless you with earning a good name through right behaviour – by being honourable, wise, moral and courageous, and dealing with integrity. I bless you with understanding that a good name is more desirable than great riches. I bless you with favour with man and God because of your good name. Favour is better than wealth; it is long-lasting and creates the platform for heart-to-heart connections that can drive positive change, and allow God's blessing on your work. Your name being held in honour brings honour to His name.

A good name is to be chosen rather than great riches, loving favor rather than silver and gold. (Proverbs 22:1)

60.

(Leader), I bless you with a heart of integrity. May integrity be one of the pillars upon which you build your leadership style and behaviour. The Oxford Dictionary describes 'integrity' as 'being honest and having strong moral principles; the state of being whole and undivided; [with] internal consistency or lack of corruption'. May your lack of appetite for corruption spill over into actively opposing corruption and dishonesty. I bless you with being an honourable judge; with the conviction of spirit to rebuke the wicked.

I bless you with answering those in your sphere of influence with honesty. The Word intimates that this is a beautiful thing: He who gives a frank answer – and, therefore, does not flatter, manipulate or play games – kisses the lips and wins the hearts of people. I bless you with finding delight and a good blessing from God because of your integrity.

But those who rebuke the wicked will have delight, and a good blessing will come upon them. He who gives a right answer kisses the lips. (Proverbs 24:25-26)

61.

(Leader), I bless you with dwelling on the high places: the places of authority, and with a clear view and perspective. I bless you with a fortress of rock as your defence as you navigate the labyrinth of leadership in your sphere of influence. I bless you with sufficient provision all your life, without having to scramble, toil or beg.

But, (Leader), according to the Word of God, these blessings come at a price. You decide whether you want to enjoy them.

I bless you with wisdom to make the right decision. I bless you with walking righteously by speaking with integrity, rejecting gain from fraud and oppression, rejecting any form of bribery, closing your ears to stories of bloodshed, and turning your eyes away from evil.

He who walks righteously and speaks uprightly, he who despises the gain of oppressions, who gestures with his hands, refusing bribes, who stops his ears from hearing of bloodshed, and shuts his eyes from seeing evil: He will dwell on high; his place of defense will be the fortress of rocks; bread will be given him, his water will be sure. (Isaiah 33:15-16)

62.

(Leader), God is not fooled. Just as surely as He forgives those who repent and change their ways, He will judge those who steadfastly persist in their evil ways. Micah laments the pervasive wickedness and the impact this has on the nation. He also conveys God's judgement. I bless you with integrity nestled deep in your core. I bless you with being surrounded by people of integrity. The results of acting contrarily are devastating – justice is perverted and when justice is perverted, the wicked reign. I bless you with a heart after light and truth.

That they may successfully do evil with both hands—the prince asks for gifts, the judge seeks a bribe, and the great man utters his evil desire; so they scheme together. (Micah 7:3)

63.

(Leader), I bless you with the private counsel of the Lord. I bless you with being upright, and having spiritual integrity and moral courage. I bless you with being and remaining honest before the Lord because He finds the devious repulsive.

For the perverse person is an abomination to the Lord, but His secret counsel is with the upright. (Proverbs 3:32)

64.

(Leader), I bless you with the desire to live in a godly manner and do the things that give God pleasure. I bless you with speaking the truth wherever you go. I bless you with judging and making decisions in truth. I bless you with pronouncing judgements or decisions that bring peace in your sphere of influence. I bless you with a pure heart and pure thoughts about those around you. I bless you with an aversion to lying and half-truths. I bless you to rule with integrity and to enjoy its fruit as God blesses you.

> *These are the things you shall do: Speak each man the truth to his neighbor; give judgment in your gates for truth, justice, and peace; let none of you think evil in your heart against your neighbor; and do not love a false oath. For all these are things that I hate,' says the Lord. (Zechariah 8:16-17)*

Chapter 7: Blessed by God

Introduction

Have you ever thought about the sheer wonder of serving a God who delights in blessing those who love and follow Him? No other religion can lay claim to that, and no wonder: our God is not about religion, is He?

He is about relationship – yesterday, today and tomorrow.

Throughout His Word, He speaks to us about His love and His character. He guides us to do those things that will propel us into His presence and He warns us about the things that obstruct His presence.

More than this, He teaches us and longs for us to *be* with Him, before we *do* for Him.

The account of Martha and Mary, where the former complained to Jesus about having to do, do, do while Mary sat at His feet, demonstrates this. His response? *And Jesus answered and said to her, "Martha, Martha, you are worried and troubled about many things. But one thing is needed, and Mary has chosen that good part, which will not be taken away from her." (Luke 10:41 and 42).*

Doing is certainly important – someone had to cook and serve, but it should never be at the expense of *being*.

In Leviticus 21:23, God gives instructions for the priestly service. He stipulates that those of the house of Aaron who have any blemishes or disfigurements are not allowed to serve at the altar. That might seem harsh, until we read further and see that each of them is, however, instructed to *"...eat of the bread of his God, both of the most holy and of the holy things"*. They were not allowed to *do*, but they still had to *be* in intimate relationship with God.

Take this relationship that God wants with us one step further. In the Priestly Blessing of Numbers 6:24-26, God instructs Aaron and his sons how they must bless the nation. It starts with "The Lord bless you...". The root of the Hebrew word for 'bless' is 'to kneel'.

Think about it: God – the Creator of heaven and earth, the One who decides where the ocean waves stop, who distributes light, guides the stars, sends lightnings, and provides for the raven (Job 38) – scripts a blessing for those who belong to Him. He not only scripts it, He kneels before us, bends towards us like we do with children, and sanctifies us with His promise of protection, kindness, love, favour and peace.

God loves to bless. It is part of His generous character.

～✿～

Press in

65.

(Leader), listen with your spirit to what the Word of God is saying to you. Be encouraged, loved and empowered to do that which you were called to do. I bless you with being a blessing wherever the Lord has placed you. If you are in right-standing with God, His blessing rests upon you. Moreover, it spills over to your sphere of influence – impacting people, productivity and profits. I bless you with being a carrier of God's blessings wherever you are.

Joseph did not have an easy road. Much of his character was formed while in prison. And he landed in prison because he chose to not give in to the temptation of sin offered by Potiphar's wife. I bless you with exhibiting the same tenacity and righteousness so that God has ample opportunity to bless those around you because of your well-formed character.

So it was, from the time that he had made him overseer of his house and all that he had, that the Lord blessed the Egyptian's house for Joseph's sake; and the blessing of the Lord was on all that he had in the house and in the field. (Genesis 39:5)

66.

(Leader), I bless you with knowing that the Lord your God has blessed you in all the work of your hands. I bless you with the comfort to know that He is intimately familiar with your path, with the difficulties, the loneliness and the times of uncertainty. I bless you with joy to realise that, even in these times, He has not forsaken you and He never will. I bless you with His all-sufficiency. I bless you with the happy prospect that, if your heart is aligned with God's, you will become greater and greater because the Lord of Hosts is with you.

"For the Lord your God has blessed you in all the work of your hand. He knows your trudging through this great wilderness. These forty years the Lord your God has been with you; you have lacked nothing." (Deuteronomy 2:7)

So David went on and became great, and the Lord God of hosts was with him. (2 Samuel 5:10 and 1 Chronicles 11:9)

67.

(Leader), in Ruth, we read a beautiful account of mutual affection and respect between a leader and his constituents. I bless you with the same. I bless you with making a conscious effort to habitually bless those under your stewardship. And I bless you with them blessing you in return, and you receiving and accepting the blessing with a heart of gratitude, as if it came from God.

Now behold, Boaz came from Bethlehem, and said to the reapers, "The Lord be with you!" And they answered him, "The Lord bless you!" (Ruth 2:4)

68.

(Leader), I bless you with the gumption to ask God to bless you with particular blessings. I bless you with the kind of relationship that is required between a child and his/her Father to boldly ask for a blessing – not because the child deserves it or is entitled to it, but simply because the child trusts that his/her Abba is a good Father who delights in blessing him/her. I bless you with joy as you extend your faith and experience the blessing of the Father.

And Jabez called on the God of Israel saying, "Oh, that You would bless me indeed, and enlarge my territory, that Your hand would be with me, and that You would keep me from evil, that I may not cause pain!" So God granted him what he requested. (1 Chronicles 4:10)

69.

(Leader), I bless you with the resilience of Joseph. For a long time, he was in a very hard place, and yet he prospered. God blessed him in every position and circumstance. I bless you with the strength and agility that can only come from God's blessing resting on a person. I bless you to thrive in the care of the Shepherd in the face of adversity. May it be said of you that you are a fruitful bough with branches running over the wall, influencing others.

> *"Joseph is a fruitful bough, a fruitful bough by a well; his branches run over the wall. The archers have bitterly grieved him, shot at him and hated him. But his bow remained in strength, and the arms of his hands were made strong by the hands of the Mighty God of Jacob (From there is the Shepherd, the Stone of Israel),... (Genesis 49:22-24)*

Chapter 8: Equipped by God

Introduction

God equips us. We might feel thoroughly inadequate for the task at hand – especially for a leadership task – and if we are not careful, that feeling debilitates us and hinders the working of God through us for that particular place and season.

He also does not equip us only spiritually; He will develop those skills and expertise we need to be able to do the work required for His bigger purpose. Our roads might seem strange and full of seemingly wrong turns, but even those He uses to equip us for what is ahead. He is faithful and steers us (even before we love Him) from position to position, from training to training, from (sometimes difficult) leader to leader; to a place where we stand in leadership. If we are sensitive, we can see the equipping signposts in neon lights.

God will do whatever is necessary for however long it takes to equip us to be of service to Him in establishing His Kingdom in the earth – no organisation or nation is excluded.

Does that mean that we will know everything technical and spiritual before He works through us? Absolutely not. We never stop learning and growing (if we choose to); that is part of the extraordinary nature of God: He equips us sufficiently so that we can make a start, and then He makes allowances for where we lack skills, information, authority, understanding, whatever..., and allows circumstances or other people to teach and guide us further.

And He is always closely involved. Closely!

It brings honour to His name when we do that for which we were created; when we grow into our full potential. Will He just leave us to it then? Of course not – He remains with us, in us, to guide us where we should go.

We want leaders and people in authority to be equipped by God. Let's ask God for it, let's bless them with what was God's idea in the first place.

> *Now may the God of peace who brought up our Lord Jesus from the dead, that great Shepherd of the sheep, through the blood of the everlasting covenant, make you complete in every good work to do His will, working in you what is well pleasing in His sight, through Jesus Christ, to whom be glory forever and ever. Amen. (Hebrews 13:20 and 21)*

∽ ⌒ ∽

Press in

70.

(Leader), align your spirit with the Spirit of God and listen to what He wants to say to you. God knows exactly what you can and cannot do. He is completely in control of your life. I bless you to yield to His guidance – even when it does not make sense. He loves you with an everlasting and all-consuming love and it is His will that you do well. I bless you with understanding this truth with your spirit, not only with your head (intellect).

I bless you with knowing that He has already equipped you for the work at hand and that He will continue to guide you. What you see as your drawbacks or weaknesses, He sees as opportunities to prove Himself strong in your favour. I bless you with supernatural faith and trust that He will teach you what to say and do in any given situation.

So the Lord said to him, "Who has made man's mouth? Or who makes the mute, the deaf, the seeing, or the blind? Have not I, the Lord? Now therefore, go, and I will be with your mouth and teach you what you shall say." (Exodus 4:11 and 12)

71.

(Leader), I bless you with recognising the tools with which you are already equipped. God did not leave you clueless at the Red Sea with hordes of enemies on your trail. He did not leave you clueless in the boardroom facing exacting shareholders requiring an explanation or solution to a challenge. He did not leave you clueless in the face of danger threatening your country, nation or family.

I bless you with clearly and creatively identifying those tools already in your possession. I bless you with faith to use those tools, trusting that God will do the rest – add to your tools, divinely intervene if necessary, give new revelation.

I bless you with the freedom of asking God for guidance in any case. He might ask you why you are crying to Him if you already know some of what needs to be done, but His guidance will come, nonetheless. I bless you with knowing God as the God who willingly guides and lavishly imparts wisdom.

And the Lord said to Moses, "Why do you cry to Me? Tell the children of Israel to go forward. But lift up your rod, and stretch out

your hand over the sea and divide it. And the children of Israel shall
go on dry ground through the midst of the sea. (Exodus 14:15-16)

72.

(Leader), I bless you because God has called you by name. I bless you to stand still at this point for a bit – have a Selah moment: I bless you with joy to revel in the fact that the living God has carved out a place specifically for you in which to have dominion; He has already nailed your name on the office door. I bless you with the Spirit of God continuing to fill you with wisdom and skill, understanding and intelligence, knowledge and all kinds of expertise.

I bless you to rejoice in the fact that you have been blessed and equipped with a number of skills, attributes, expertise to be able to do what needs to be done in this season. I bless you to rest in the knowledge that God is a God of excellence. He exudes it and He expects it from you – what's more, He has equipped you to rise up to a standard of excellence.

"See, I have called by name Bezalel the son of Uri, the son of Hur, of the tribe of Judah. And I have filled him with the Spirit of God, in wisdom, in understanding, in knowledge, and in all manner of workmanship, to design artistic works, to work in gold, in silver, in bronze,… (Exodus 31:2-4)

73.

(Leader), I bless you with a strong team of people – whether employees, service providers, counsellors, advisors – around you. I bless you with God Himself sending you the right people; those whom He has already equipped for the work to be done. I bless you with being surrounded by wise people. Through you, I bless them with the ability to tap into the skills and knowledge they already have, and also with a willingness and eagerness to grow and develop further. Because this is also God's will.

"And I, indeed I, have appointed with him Aholiab the son of Ahisamach, of the tribe of Dan; and I have put wisdom in the hearts of all the gifted artisans, that they may make all that I have commanded you. (Exodus 31:6)

74.

(Leader), I bless you with passion for your work and position. I bless those whom the Lord placed around you with passion for their work and responsibilities. I bless you with not taking the Lord's equipping for granted – as if your skills and talents are a random occurrence – He assigned them to you specifically. I bless you with being amazed at how your particular design and the flavour of your personality and background enhance your abilities and make it unique: No one else can do the work the way you do. I bless you with having your heart stirred up to get the job done, and to do it well.

And all the women whose hearts stirred with wisdom spun yarn of goats' hair. (Exodus 35:26)

Chapter 9: Encouraged by God

Introduction

Have you ever observed parents at an athletics meeting, watching their children race against others, as well as trying to beat their own previous record? It is a sight to behold. Arms gesticulating, eyes fixated, mouths bellowing advice and praise, bodies bent slightly forward in readiness to jump on the track themselves, if more encouragement is required.

I think that is how God and the cloud of witnesses surround us while we are running this race (Hebrews 12:1).

I take great comfort in knowing that God is outside of time: He sees the beginning and the end, He knows us inside out. He knows what we are fighting against – our own weaknesses, hang-ups, generational issues, circumstances and demonic influences.

But, praise His name, He is not deterred by any of that. He will accomplish His purposes. And He continuously encourages us not to give up, to trust Him, and to allow Him to help us get closer and closer to Him.

Now to Him who is able to do exceedingly abundantly above all that we ask or think, according to the power that works in us, to Him be glory in the church by Christ Jesus to all generations, forever and ever. Amen. (Ephesians 3:20 and 21)

People in authority are still people. They get tired. They feel insecure. They sometimes stumble under the weight of the responsibility they carry. They fear not being able to live up to the (sometimes unreasonable) expectations of others. They do not always have all the answers, and few have the confidence (and humility) to say so and seek help. They know criticism is only a decision away. They also know that they cannot trust every compliment. Often, they cannot be sure that the hand giving the pat on the back is not also holding a knife. Some decisions are very difficult to make – especially if leaders really care about their people.

They, like everyone else, need to be encouraged. No one does this better than our heavenly Father.

***

Press in

75.

(Leader), let your spirit attend to the Word of God for you. A major source of encouragement from God is His promises and dreams for us. I bless you with searching out His promises in His Word. I bless you with a relationship with God that is intimate. One where you hear His promises for you in your heart during your times of fellowship with Him.

I bless you with your dreams being aligned with His dreams for you. I bless you with divine appointments, where God can use His children to share His promises with you. I bless you with the promises finding their way into your heart. I bless you with being able to give expression to His promises, to make them real and to stir encouragement within you. I bless you to know that He is with you; that He guards over you; and that He guarantees not to leave you until He has done what He has promised.

Then he dreamed, and behold, a ladder was set up on the earth, and its top reached to heaven; and there the angels of God were ascending and descending on it. And behold, the Lord stood above it and said: "I am the Lord God of Abraham your father and the God of Isaac; the land on which you lie I will give to you and your descendants. Also your descendants shall be as the dust of the earth; you shall spread abroad to the west and the east, to the north and the south; and in you and in your seed all the families of the earth shall be blessed. Behold, I am with you and will keep you wherever you go, and will bring you back to this land; for I will not leave you until I have done what I have spoken to you." Then Jacob awoke from his sleep and said, "Surely the Lord is in this place, and I did not know it." (Genesis 28:12-16)

76.

(Leader), God knows the thoughts and plans He has for you. I bless you with His promises for you: His thoughts and plans for welfare and peace. I bless you with His hope living inside you. I bless you with the belief that everything will work out in accordance with His plans for you. I bless you with the fruit of seeing all He has given you: that you will call on Him, pray to Him and be heard by Him. I bless you with seeking Him, enquiring of Him and requiring Him as your vital necessity. I bless you with finding Him, if you search for Him with all your heart.

For I know the thoughts that I think toward you, says the Lord, thoughts of peace and not of evil, to give you a future and a hope. Then you will call upon Me and go and pray to Me, and I will listen to you.

And you will seek Me and find Me, when you search for Me with all your heart. (Jeremiah 29:11-13)

77.

(Leader), I bless you with remembering the promises God has made to you – whether by speaking to you directly, through His Word or through others. I bless you with praying these promises back to God like Jacob did. Not because God has forgotten, but because it builds your faith and encourages you when His promises pass from your heart through your lips to His ears. I bless you to verbalise your faith in the God who promised. I bless you to allow God's promises to encourage you and give you hope.

For You said, 'I will surely treat you well, and make your descendants as the sand of the sea, which cannot be numbered for multitude.' (Genesis 32:12)

78.

(Leader), I bless you with believing God's promises, and trusting in and relying on God. I bless you with a confident expectation and hope in God. I bless you with spiritual security. Be encouraged: you will be nourished like a tree planted by the waters. You will not fear the heat when it comes. Your leaves – that which you offer and which you are called to do – will remain green and moist. You will not be anxious or worried when the going gets tough for a season, for your hope is in God.

Blessed is the man who trusts in the Lord, and whose hope is the Lord. For he shall be like a tree planted by the waters, which spreads out its roots by the river, and will not fear when heat comes; but its leaf will be green, and will not be anxious in the year of drought, nor will cease from yielding fruit. (Jeremiah 17:7 and 8)

79.

(Leader), I bless you with confidence and courage. Remember that God will make good on His promises to you. All that is required from you is to have courage and be obedient. I bless you with a heart set to obey all that God has instructed. I bless you with being aligned to His Kingdom principles. Then you will be successful wherever you go, and prosper. I bless you with a hunger for the Word of God and a willingness to use it as your navigation system. I bless you with making your own way prosperous as you follow God's Word. Be courageous! The Lord God is with you wherever you go.

Be strong and of good courage, for to this people you shall divide as an inheritance the land which I swore to their fathers to give them. Only be strong and very courageous, that you may observe to do according to all the law which Moses My servant commanded you; do not turn from it to the right hand or to the left, that you may prosper wherever you go. This Book of the Law shall not depart from your mouth, but you shall meditate in it day and night, that you may observe to do according to all that is written in it. For then you will make your way prosperous, and then you will have good success. Have I not commanded you? Be strong and of good courage; do not be afraid, nor be dismayed, for the Lord your God is with you wherever you go. (Joshua 1:6-9)

80.

(Leader), I bless you with looking into God's mirror and seeing yourself the way He sees you. Gideon did not think of himself as a brave man, yet that was the second thing the Angel of the Lord drew his attention to.

He first encouraged him by affirming that God was with him. Then he called him by one of the characteristics and benefits which flows from having God on your side. I bless you with being brave. Whether you face adversity or difficult decisions, are breaking new ground, or have to walk the tightrope between family and work responsibilities – be brave, the Lord is with you.

Be blessed with an authenticity in your relationship with God, where you have the freedom to be honest about not understanding why things happen the way they do. God is not intimidated by our questions. In the Lord's response to Gideon's not-too-gracious comment, it is almost as if He is saying, 'See, I said you were brave: now, go save a nation!' I bless you, (Leader), with encouragement from the Most High who has sent you.

And the Angel of the Lord appeared to him, and said to him, "The Lord is with you, you mighty man of valor!" Gideon said to Him, "O my lord, if the Lord is with us, why then has all this happened to us? And where are all His miracles which our fathers told us about, saying, 'Did not the Lord bring us up from Egypt?' But now the Lord has forsaken us and delivered us into the hands of the Midianites." Then the Lord turned to him and said, "Go in this might of yours, and you shall save Israel from the hand of the Midianites. Have I not sent you?" (Judges 6:12-14)

81.

(Leader), I bless you with being blameless before God. I bless you with being fearless. Be encouraged that the Lord is your confidence. He is the one keeping you from being trapped in a place or situation that is not from Him.

Do not be afraid of sudden terror, nor of trouble from the wicked when it comes; For the Lord will be your confidence, and will keep your foot from being caught. (Proverbs 3:25 and 26)

82.

(Leader), I bless you with being clothed by the Spirit of God with a mantle of empowerment. Be encouraged that the Lord has dressed you with whatever you need to rally your people, as well as people from other 'clans' that the Lord has ordained to fight alongside you, and to face whatever battles come your way.

But the Spirit of the Lord came upon Gideon; then he blew the trumpet, and the Abiezrites gathered behind him. (Judges 6:34)

83.

(Leader), I bless you with an internal compass for navigation on the road of the righteous. Hear the encouragement of the Lord: the way of those who live in moral and spiritual integrity is smooth and level. I bless you with God levelling the road for you and making a way where you thought there could be no way. The one who is in right-standing with God can do mighty things!

The way of the just is uprightness; O Most Upright, You weigh the path of the just. (Isaiah 26:7)

(Leader), I bless you with the encouragement that, if you follow hard after God, you will be able to do mighty things. Daniel was a righteous man; his enemies knew this and they knew that the only way they could do him harm would be to challenge the object of his affection – his God. Daniel knew about the decree to worship the king. Was he intimidated? Not at all. He kept to his routine of openly praying to his God three times a day.

I bless you with the same resolve not to compromise, but to swim upstream in obedience to God and out of love for Him. Even when he was thrown into the lions' den, he did not recant. He knew His God was well able to save him even from that seemingly impossible place.

I bless your testimony of God's goodness. May it stir the hearts of those you submit to; may they also, like the king, bless you with the favour and protection of your God. I bless you with being ready in season and out of season to testify to God's goodness and His divine intervention in your life.

I bless you with being innocent before God, so that His encouragement to do mighty things may find expression in your life.

Then these men said, "We shall not find any charge against this Daniel unless we find it against him concerning the law of his God." Now when Daniel knew that the writing was signed, he went home. And in his upper room, with his windows open toward Jerusalem, he knelt down on his knees three times that day, and prayed and gave thanks before his God, as was his custom since early days. So the king gave the command, and they brought Daniel and cast him into the den of lions. But the king spoke, saying to Daniel, "Your God, whom you serve continually, He will deliver you." My God sent His angel and shut the lions' mouths, so that they have not hurt me, because I was found innocent before Him; and also, O king, I have done no wrong before you." (Daniel 6:5, 10, 16 and 22)

85.

(Leader), I bless you with Habakkuk's anthem of faith – tie it to your heart, use it as your banner, rejoice in the encouragement it brings and in the promise of accomplishing great things. The Lord God is your strength, (Leader); He is your source of courage and your invincible army. He has made your feet steady and sure like those of a deer. He causes you to walk with spiritual confidence on your high places, and your places of authority, challenge and responsibility.

The Lord God is my strength; He will make my feet like deer's feet, and He will make me walk on my high hills. (Habakkuk 3:19)

Chapter 10: Guided by God

Introduction

I cannot help returning to this point: What other religion or faith has as its 'proprietor' a god that is willing to – and insists on – guiding his followers? A god who is happy to say, 'Here you need to turn left'; 'Be on the lookout for that nasty trap'; 'Why don't you rest a while before we continue?'; 'If you do it like this, you will benefit by…'; 'Ask Me, I want to help'?

Our God does.

He delights in us asking for His guidance and He honours such a request every time. He values that we wait for His guidance; a difficult thing in our 'instant', western way of thinking. He gives guidance in incredible detail – just look at His instructions for the building of the tabernacle and the temple. He guides how we are to do our work and He is the Master Strategist, willing to guide the strategic direction of companies and nations. He also guides by teaching and empowering us to solve problems creatively, and with His blessing.

John 16:13 says, *However, when He, the Spirit of truth, has come, He will guide you into all truth; for He will not speak on His own authority, but whatever He hears He will speak; and He will tell you things to come.*

If we are to pray for God's will to be done on earth as it is in heaven, for His Kingdom principles to be made manifest on earth, then surely we will need leaders who are led and guided by God's Spirit!

We need leaders (and must be leaders) who recognise their need to be guided by the Most High God; delight in His guidance; are willing to persevere in waiting for His guidance; seek and follow His guidance in every aspect of their lives, not only where it is comfortable; and are obedient and teachable.

The Spirit of Truth will guide in truth, as the Father wills.

***

Press in

86.

(Leader), listen with your spirit to what God's Spirit is saying to you. We not only need God's guidance in difficult times, or when we know we do not have the answers. We also need it when circumstances seem good. The Israelites found that out the hard way. God had instructed them to destroy a number of heathen nations (Deuteronomy 20:17). In the book of Joshua, they are tricked by the Gibeonites into making a covenant with them. According to this covenant, Israel had to protect the Gibeonites and fight for them. They agreed to this without asking God's counsel and obtained for themselves a thorn in the flesh.

I bless you with valuing God's guidance in everything you do, in every season of your life. Ask for His guidance. I bless you with remembering God's guidance and instructions, and with being obedient. I bless you with not being lulled into complacency or comfort by the appearance of situations, but to always keep the Lord before you, ready to act on His slightest unction.

> *Then the men of Israel took some of their provisions; but they did not ask counsel of the Lord. (Joshua 9:14)*

87.

(Leader), I bless you with being diligent and constant in seeking God's guidance. I bless you with valuing His guidance more than your own knowledge or expertise, especially in adversity. I bless you with King Hezekiah's resolve to seek God's face the moment a threat comes. He heard about trouble and immediately sought God's face. He received the letter from the enemy and immediately went to God with it. And God was waiting. I bless you with stepping into God's throne room with boldness and confidence that He is ready to guide you.

> *And so it was, when King Hezekiah heard it, that he tore his clothes, covered himself with sackcloth, and went into the house of the Lord. And Hezekiah received the letter from the hand of the messengers, and read it; and Hezekiah went up to the house of the Lord, and spread it before the Lord. (Isaiah 37:1 and 14)*

88.

Oh, (Leader), that you would grasp your need for guidance from the Most High! I bless you with knowing God, searching for Him and realising your need of Him in all your affairs. I bless you with the wisdom that flows from knowing God and His guidance. May you prosper in Him, and may those who the Lord has entrusted to you be safe and secure under your leading.

For the shepherds have become dull-hearted, and have not sought the Lord; therefore they shall not prosper, and all their flocks shall be scattered. (Jeremiah 10:21)

89.

(Leader), I bless you with earnestly inviting the Lord to build your house. It might be the house of your family, your business or your country. Whatever you are building, know that it will only reach its potential and be safe if the Lord builds it – if your guidance comes from Him. You might be able to put together quite a nice house by yourself, but it will never be as good as what He had in store for you and the slightest wind, whether natural or economic, will cause it to collapse.

I bless you with cultivating the habit of asking God to build the house and taking your lead from the Master Builder. I bless you with benefiting from His perfect perspective. May you build according to His plumbline (Amos 7).

Unless the Lord builds the house, they labor in vain who build it; unless the Lord guards the city, the watchman stays awake in vain. (Psalm 127:1)

90.

(Leader), I bless you with perseverance as you wait on the Lord. I bless you with an expectation to hear and receive from Him what you need, exactly when you need it. I bless you with the new strength promised in His Word when you wait on Him; renewed power; and renewed perspective as you rise up to be close to God and to see things from His viewpoint. I bless you with energy and strength to do that which He guides you to do.

Wait on Him – He will come through for you at the appointed time.

Do not be like Saul who disobeyed by not waiting for Samuel to bring him God's guidance (1 Samuel 13:8-14). He looked at his deteriorating circumstances and decided to take matters into his own hands. When Samuel finally arrived – in God's timing – it was to tell Saul that his kingdom would fail because of this act of disobedience. Gird your loins and wait on the Lord until He speaks!

> *But those who wait on the Lord shall renew their strength; they shall mount up with wings like eagles, they shall run and not be weary, they shall walk and not faint. (Isaiah 40:31)*

91.

(Leader), I bless you with an expansive trust in God to follow His guiding, even when it does not make sense to you. God sent Elijah to a widow to support him during the drought. Perhaps Elijah had a fleeting concern at the prospect, or perhaps he had no doubt whatsoever that God had sufficient provision in place already; the Word does not say. It says that upon their introduction, she gave him a graphic description of her situation and, according to her human reasoning, her and her son's imminent death by famine. Not too encouraging. Elijah was not deterred. He knew His God had guided him there. He heard from God what he should tell the widow and delivered the instruction. She obeyed and had enough for her household and Elijah until God opened the heavens again.

I bless you, (Leader), with the trust in God's faithfulness that Elijah had. I bless you with following His instructions to the letter and not being deterred by what the situation looks like. I bless you with hearing God's details – He specified the what, the how and the how long.

I bless you with the faith of the widow who trusted what the man of God said to her; and her obedience, which led to a miracle that she had certainly not been expecting earlier that day!

> *"Arise, go to Zarephath, which belongs to Sidon, and dwell there. See, I have commanded a widow there to provide for you." So he arose and went to Zarephath. And when he came to the gate of the city, indeed a widow was there gathering sticks. And he called to her and said, "Please bring me a little water in a cup, that I may drink." And as she was going to get it, he called to her and said, "Please bring me a morsel of bread in your hand." So she said, "As the Lord your God lives, I do not have bread, only a handful of flour in a bin, and a little oil in a jar; and see, I am gathering a couple of sticks that I may go in and prepare it for myself and my son, that we may eat it, and die." And Elijah said to her, "Do not fear; go and do as you have said, but make me a small cake from it first, and bring it to me; and afterward make some for yourself and your son. For thus says the Lord God of Israel: 'The bin of flour shall not be used up, nor shall the jar of oil run dry, until the day the Lord sends rain on the earth.' " So she went away and did according to the word of Elijah; and she and he and her household ate for many days. (1 Kings 17:9-15)*

92.

(Leader), I bless you with the joy of experiencing God's guidance and the joy of Him partnering with you to accomplish His will. Nothing is hidden from God. Nothing takes Him by surprise. He is well able to guide you out of the most distressing of times. In Daniel's case, his life and those of his friends and colleagues were at stake because of a near impossible request by his 'boss'.

I bless you with praising God's name for His mercy and wisdom extended to you. I bless you with seeing God for Who He is: all-powerful, all-knowing, generous, light.

> *Then the secret was revealed to Daniel in a night vision. So Daniel blessed the God of heaven. Daniel answered and said: "Blessed be the name of God forever and ever, for wisdom and might are His. And He changes the times and the seasons; He removes kings and raises up kings; He gives wisdom to the wise and knowledge to those who have understanding. He reveals deep and secret things; He knows what is in the darkness, and light dwells with Him. "I thank You and praise You, O God of my fathers; You have given me wisdom and might, and have now made known to me what we asked of You, for You have made known to us the king's demand." (Daniel 2:19-23)*

93.

(Leader), I bless you with the anointing of Issachar, to understand the times. This anointing comes from God and, with it, the knowledge of what you should be doing in these times. I bless you with God's guidance throughout every season in your position of authority. I bless you with the right followers, who will follow your lead as God guides.

> *...of the sons of Issachar who had understanding of the times, to know what Israel ought to do, their chiefs were two hundred; and all their brethren were at their command;...(1 Chronicles 12:32)*

94.

(Leader), I bless you with accepting the Lord's strategic guidance. One of the most difficult things is to move from a good place to a new place. I bless you with the wisdom and discernment to know when God is moving you to a next level, a new season with new ground to conquer. I bless you with the assurance that it is God's will and plan to share His plans with you, so that you are prepared and can follow His guidance in establishing something new. I bless you with the ability to let go of what has been and not to make idols of old successes (or failures). I bless you with seeing how He makes a road for you where you could never have imagined.

"Do not remember the former things, nor consider the things of old. Behold, I will do a new thing, now it shall spring forth; shall you not know it? I will even make a road in the wilderness and rivers in the desert. (Isaiah 43:18 and 19)

95.

(Leader), I bless you with remembering that God is outside of time: He sees the beginning from the end and the end from the beginning. He knows the best way for you to go, the best tactical approach for you to take. Ask Him for the everlasting (ancient) paths: those paths where His goodness and His principles may be found. I bless you with walking on those everlasting paths and finding rest for your soul. Do not be foolish like the Israelites who would not follow God's guidance. Walk in His good, joyful and bountiful way.

Thus says the Lord: "Stand in the ways and see, and ask for the old paths, where the good way is, and walk in it; then you will find rest for your souls. But they said, 'We will not walk in it.' (Jeremiah 6:16)

96.

(Leader), I bless you with being properly instructed and taught by God – according to the Word. God knows what is needed for your business and your constituents. He knows the strategy you should employ to reach your objectives. In fact, He knows what your objectives should be. He is willing to be involved and, as your relationship with Him grows, you will see that He has changed places with you – He is running the business and you are involved!

I bless you with being guided by God regarding when you should sow what, and how and when you should prepare the ground. His counsel is wonderful and His wisdom great. I bless you with a personal experience of both.

Does the plowman keep plowing all day to sow? Does he keep turning his soil and breaking the clods? When he has leveled its surface, does he not sow the black cumin and scatter the cummin, plant the wheat in rows, the barley in the appointed place, and the spelt in its place? For He instructs him in right judgment, his God teaches him. For the black cummin is not threshed with a threshing sledge, nor is a cartwheel rolled over the cummin; but the black cummin is beaten out with a stick, and the cummin with a rod. Bread flour must be ground; therefore he does not thresh it forever, break it with his cartwheel, or crush it with his horsemen. This also comes from the Lord of hosts, Who is wonderful in counsel and excellent in guidance. (Isaiah 28:24-29)

97.

(Leader), I bless you with seeking to be taught by God, not only in how to do things and lead your people, but also in what not to do. I bless you with the strength of character and resolve to put an end to those practices that do not carry His blessing, and which might bring a curse instead. I bless you with being a quick and willing learner.

I bless you to move on quickly from lessons learnt, and not to dwell on past mistakes or blatant unrighteousness. If you have brought these before God, they are dealt with and you are restored.

Teach me what I do not see; if I have done iniquity, I will do no more? (Job 34:32)

98.

(Leader), I bless you with taking God at His Word. He says that He is your God. He teaches you to profit. He leads you in the way that you should go. Can anything be clearer than that? I bless you with grabbing hold of this amazing truth – God is the one Who will teach you what you should know in any given situation, and the one Who will guide you where you should go. I bless you with leaving no stone unturned to be in His perfect will for your life – and the lives of those He has entrusted to you.

Thus says the Lord, your Redeemer, the Holy One of Israel: "I am the Lord your God, Who teaches you to profit, Who leads you by the way you should go. (Isaiah 48:17)

(Leader), I bless you with the kind of relationship with God where you are honest about your fears and insecurities. Too often, the world's expectation is that leaders must have it all together. That is not God's expectation. He knows you; He knows full well in which areas you are struggling. If He knows, why should you tell Him? Because it is tremendously liberating to acknowledge your (perceived) weaknesses to the Creator of heaven and earth; in some way, it takes the sting out. Perhaps that is because God can shine His light on this issue you have been trying to keep in the dark and He can show you how the enemy of your soul, the one who continually plots against your rule, has been lying to you.

I bless you with peace. Peace and rest in the knowledge and truth that He is the One Who appointed you; He teaches you what to say because He knows what needs to be heard. I bless you with remaining tranquil, even when those you are speaking to are ungracious or antagonistic. Trust God that if you are in His will, you are under His protection and can expect His deliverance.

> Then said I: "Ah, Lord God! Behold, I cannot speak, for I am a youth." But the Lord said to me: "Do not say, 'I am a youth,' For you shall go to all to whom I send you, and whatever I command you, you shall speak. Do not be afraid of their faces, for I am with you to deliver you," says the Lord. (Jeremiah 1:6-8)

100.

(Leader), you have easy access to the King of kings. I bless you with calling on Him daily, throughout the day. I bless you with calling to God with your praises and thanksgiving, with your questions and with your concerns. He promises to answer you. More than that – He promises you a conversation! I bless you with living with God in perpetual wonder at what He is showing you and teaching you. I bless you with looking forward each day to finding what He has chosen to reveal to you for that day.

'Call to Me, and I will answer you, and show you great and mighty things, which you do not know.' (Jeremiah 33:3)

101.

(Leader), I bless you with wisdom in dealing with your people. I bless you with understanding and mercy. I bless you with knowing where to draw the line, and how to bring correction which is not only aligned with the official regulations, but also with God's principles.

I bless you with receiving strategy from the Lord for dealing with those who take no responsibility for their errors. I bless you with discernment from the Word to identify the scoffers and the wise in your sphere of influence. The scoffers are those who scorn guidance and who are quick to pass the buck. The wise are those who take correction well and value the opportunity to learn.

I bless you with weeding out the scoffers and surrounding yourself with the wise. I bless you to be instrumental in helping the wise become wiser and increasing their learning. Then you will leave an honourable legacy.

Do not correct a scoffer, lest he hate you; rebuke a wise man, and he will love you. Give instruction to a wise man, and he will be still wiser; teach a just man, and he will increase in learning. (Proverbs 9:8-9)

102.

(Leader), I bless you with allowing no room for the hate of the scoffer. I bless you with the perfect time – God's timing – to bring punishment to bear on the scoffer, so that the observers will also learn from it and become wise. I bless you with continued growth in your business, or whatever your position of authority entails because, as the wise are instructed, knowledge increases.

When the scoffer is punished, the simple is made wise; but when the wise is instructed, he receives knowledge. (Proverbs 21:11)

103.

(Leader), it might not be that easy to let go of those who leave chaos in their wake, or those who harm the place under your stewardship. I bless you with wisdom to do this correctly and quickly. I bless you with razor-sharp discernment to identify those who cause strife and dishonour – sometimes they hide behind false smiles and seemingly busy schedules. I bless you with receiving God's guidance on the best solution for you and them because He cares for them too.

Cast out the scoffer, and contention will leave; yes, strife and reproach will cease. (Proverbs 22:10)

Chapter 11: Importance of good counsel

Introduction

God did not mean for any of us to 'go it alone'. He created us in fellowship from the start, first husband and wife, then families, communities and nations.

His Word counsels us to make sure that we are surrounded by righteous counsel. We know from experience that He often speaks through these counsellors, especially if there is some hindrance between us and Him, and He needs to get a word of wisdom or correction to us. Or sometimes, He chooses to speak through other people because of the journey He has undertaken with them and He wants to establish something through them.

> *Now I myself am confident concerning you, my brethren, that you also are full of goodness, filled with all knowledge, able also to admonish one another. (Romans 15:14)*

We rarely just storm ahead into making decisions or starting projects: mostly, we would ask those we trust for advice.

> *Or what king, going to make war against another king, does not sit down first and consider whether he is able with ten thousand to meet him who comes against him with twenty thousand? (Luke 14:31)*

A person in authority is no different. On the contrary – we can probably trace a number of good and bad decisions to the advisors and counsellors of those in authority.

As we appeal to God to appoint godly leaders, to transform current leaders into His likeness, to give them wisdom, to align their behaviour with His Kingdom principles, to equip them, to encourage them, to guide them, and to appoint godly counsellors and advisors around them, so, too, we have to pray for those counsellors.

❧

Press in

104.

(Leader), tune in your spirit to hear what the Spirit of God wants to say to you. I bless you with counsellors who have your best interests at heart, and are bold enough to speak into your life and bring correction, where needed. Moses had such a counsellor in his father-in-law. He saw that Moses' leadership style would not only result in harm to Moses, but was also hard on the people. He advised Moses to appoint righteous people to help him (and introduced Moses to the art of delegation).

I bless you with counsellors who are competent, fear God, are filled with integrity and hate dishonest gain.

I bless you with the wisdom to draw on the right counsellors at the right time – each counsellor has a specific gifting from God: I bless you to identify the gifts around you and to draw on that.

So when Moses' father-in-law saw all that he did for the people, he said, "What is this thing that you are doing for the people? Why do you alone sit, and all the people stand before you from morning until evening?" "Moreover you shall select from all the people able men, such as fear God, men of truth, hating covetousness; and place such over them to be rulers of thousands, rulers of hundreds, rulers of fifties, and rulers of tens." (Exodus 18:14 and 21)

105.

(Leader), King David had just informed his wife Bathsheba that their son Solomon would be king. The very next thing he did was to inform his closest counsellors. I bless you, (Leader), with having trustworthy and experienced counsellors close to you. I bless you with calling on the right selection of counsellors for the right purpose.

King David's selection on that particular occasion was interesting: a priest who ministered to God and man, a prophet who brought the Word of God and a warrior known for his mighty deeds. The priest and prophet were there to conduct the proceedings of anointing Solomon as king, and the warrior was there for his protection. I bless you with rightly discerning which functions are required to attain the vision.

And King David said, "Call to me Zadok the priest, Nathan the prophet, and Benaiah the son of Jehoiada." So they came before the king. The king also said to them, "Take with you the servants of your lord, and have Solomon my son ride on my own mule, and take him down to Gihon. There let Zadok the priest and Nathan the prophet anoint him king over Israel; and blow the horn, and say, 'Long live King Solomon!' (1 Kings 1:32-34)

106.

(Leader), I bless you with wisdom to follow the right advice. I bless you with such a close relationship with God that your counsellors will only serve to give confirmation, or to add additional details as decided by God. In this way, your ears will be practised to discern counsel that does not bear God's blessing.

Young king Rehoboam was entreated by his people to lighten the burden Solomon had placed on them. When the king asked the older counsellors for advice, they gave him wise counsel because they knew the mood of the people. When he then asked his friends who had grown up with him, however, they gave him rash advice, motivated by the need to prove a point, not by what was best for the nation. While this was from God, it does illustrate the necessity of godly counsellors.

I bless you with the insight to understand that the best counsellors are not necessarily your friends. Be brave and visionary to select counsellors who might be completely different from you. Ask God's guidance: He knows who will complement your skills.

And they spoke to him, saying, "If you will be a servant to these people today, and serve them, and answer them, and speak good words to them, then they will be your servants forever." (1 Kings 12:7)

107.

(Leader), I bless you with not taking the necessity of wise counsellors for granted. I bless you with experiencing your hands being strengthened by the right people around you. I bless you with victory and safety because righteous people are speaking into your life. I bless you with steering your ship on a sure course. I bless your plans: may they be established and successful because of wise counsel.

For by wise counsel you will wage your own war, and in a multitude of counselors there is safety. (Proverbs 24:6)

Where there is no [wise, intelligent] guidance, the people fall [and go off course like a ship without a helm], But in the abundance of [wise and godly] counselors there is victory. (Proverbs 11:14 AMP)

Without consultation and wise advice, plans are frustrated, but with many counselors they are established and succeed. (Proverbs 15:22 AMP)

108.

(Leader), I bless you with ears that hear the warning of the Lord, and a spirit and soul that are willing to guard against veering off the right road. Listen to the consequence of knowingly walking in the counsel of the wicked. Notice the effect it has on the nation:

"You shall sow, but not reap; you shall tread the olives, but not anoint yourselves with oil; and make sweet wine, but not drink wine. For the statutes of Omri are kept; all the works of Ahab's house are done; and you walk in their counsels, that I may make you a desolation, and your inhabitants a hissing. Therefore you shall bear the reproach of My people." (Micah 6:15 and 16)

I bless you, (Leader), with a heart after God. I bless you with counsellors with hearts after God. I bless you to make drastic corrections when you encounter behaviour that is condemned by God, in your sphere of influence.

Chapter 12: Leaving a legacy

Introduction

God's Word has much to say about inheritance. The passing down from one generation to the next of material things, as well as spiritual blessings (or curses), is a principle we cannot ignore.

We, also, have an inborn desire to leave a legacy of value: to not just fade into oblivion, but to leave something that would make a difference even after we are gone.

Succession plans for leadership are prominent around the world and are linked to benefits such as 'sustainability', 'continuity' and 'retention', to name a few. God also values succession plans – just read the clear instructions to the kings of old regarding who their successors should be.

Let's pray for our leaders' legacies. When transformation comes, and our communities and nations are living in peace because of righteous leadership (because we did our part by praying!), our work is not over – if the enemy of our souls lost the battle in this generation, he will try again in the next.

Not only do we want our leaders to leave a legacy that is blessed and smiled on by God, but we also want subsequent leaders to look after that inheritance by walking in their godly footsteps. They have, after all, been ordained by God.

In Him also we have obtained an inheritance, being predestined according to the purpose of Him who works all things according to the counsel of His will,...(Ephesians 1:11)

***

Press in

109.

(Leader), listen to what the spirit of God wants to say to you. I bless you with everything you need, from a close relationship with God, to material blessings, spiritual blessings and Godly interventions – whatever! – to leave a praiseworthy legacy to those coming after you. I bless you that it will be said of you that they found rich, good pasture; a wide, clean, peaceful land; and a better place than before because of your investment in leading your people and executing your responsibilities with excellence, aligned with God.

And they found rich, good pasture, and the land was broad, quiet, and peaceful; for some Hamites formerly lived there. (1 Chronicles 4:40)

110.

(Leader), the book of Numbers features a beautiful example of the changing of the guard. I bless you with a successor who has the indwelling Spirit of God. I bless you with finding an opportunity to establish your successor in the sight of those they will be leading by highlighting a key responsibility of their position. It is more beneficial for your people to see you openly showing support for your successor than you leaving the one day and your successor walking in cold the next. I bless you with the generosity of spirit to openly honour your successor, so that those they lead will make a quick transition.

And the Lord said to Moses: "Take Joshua the son of Nun with you, a man in whom is the Spirit, and lay your hand on him; set him before Eleazar the priest and before all the congregation, and inaugurate him in their sight. And you shall give some of your authority to him, that all the congregation of the children of Israel may be obedient. (Numbers 27:18-20)

111.

(Leader), moving into the next season of your life can be difficult and you might be tempted to either 'move on' as soon as possible, or to hold onto the reins. I bless you with the grace to think about your successor with the heart of a steward. See it as part of your legacy to impart what wisdom you can and then graciously bow out. I bless you with making an effort to have a private conversation with your successor, to bless them with whatever pearls of wisdom the Lord lays on your heart.

Now Joshua the son of Nun was full of the spirit of wisdom, for Moses had laid his hands on him; so the children of Israel heeded him, and did as the Lord had commanded Moses. (Deuteronomy 34:9)

Chapter 13: The example of Nehemiah

Introduction

The book of Nehemiah might very well be the Leadership 101 of the Word. It is rich in imagery regarding the leadership walk and offers magnificent views of all the actors in a leader's story — vision, followers, superiors, opposition, strategy, implementation and impact, among others.

The blessings that follow give a snapshot of the treasures buried in the book of Nehemiah. There are many more to be mined, and I would encourage you to study this book and identify those jewels you can appropriate for yourself. Look specifically at every situation, the opposition's response, and Nehemiah's response to either the situation or the opposition. The thread of God-focused leadership is pure gold.

Press in

112.

(Leader), listen with your spirit to what the Spirit of God wants to teach you and how He wants to bless you with the account of Nehemiah.

While in exile, Nehemiah served the Persian king in the castle of Shushan. He heard from a relative that it was not going well with those who had escaped exile and were still living in the destroyed Jerusalem. His reaction to this news was to mourn and fast. He wept for days and prayed constantly to God.

(Leader), I bless you with a close relationship with God: one where you are completely honest before Him, in brokenness and in praise; a relationship characterised by a deep reverence for Him and the confidence to approach Him on behalf of others.

I said, "I beseech You, O Lord God of heaven, the great and awesome God, who preserves the covenant and lovingkindness for those who love Him and keep His commandments, (Nehemiah 1:5 - NASB)

113.

(Leader), I bless you with a humble heart before God: a heart of compassion and intercession to stand in the gap for your people before God. I bless you with a revelation of the power of identificational repentance, where you willingly identify with the sin of your people and ask for forgiveness, so that God can heal and restore. I bless you with the honesty to list the sins by name and allow God's light to shine on them.

I bless you with remembering the promises in God's Word and those He made to you personally. God did not forget those promises, but it stirs our faith and increases our strength to repeat them.

Let Your ear now be attentive and Your eyes open to hear the prayer of Your servant which I am praying before You now, day and night, on behalf of the sons of Israel Your servants, confessing the sins of the sons of Israel which we have sinned against You; I and my father's house have sinned. We have acted very corruptly against You and have not kept the commandments, nor the statutes, nor the ordinances which You commanded Your servant Moses. Remember the word which You commanded Your servant Moses, saying, 'If you are unfaithful I will scatter you among the peoples; but if you return to Me and keep My commandments and do them, though those of you who have been scattered were in the most remote part of the heavens, I will gather them from there and will bring them to the place where I have chosen to cause My name to dwell.' They are Your servants and Your people whom You redeemed by Your great power and by Your strong hand. (Nehemiah 1:6-10 - NASB)

114.

Nehemiah was a cup bearer. While a privileged position in the king's court, this was not exactly a picture of leadership. Until ... Nehemiah's position changed drastically when he heard the news about his people, allowed compassion to settle in his heart, and rent his heart before God in repentance and supplication. He went from butler to visionary. An enormous vision which would catapult him into a position of leadership in one prayer.

I bless you, (Leader), to increase in favour with God and man. I bless you with a vision that is a carbon copy of the vision that God has for your particular situation (Psalm 37:4). Then He will hear and grant your request, and will cause your superiors to bestow favour on you. I bless you with the favour to be able to delegate upwards, like Nehemiah did when he asked the king for administrative assistance! I bless you with being established in your position of leadership because it is from God. I bless you with the good hand of God on you.

Then the king said to me, "What would you request?" So I prayed to the God of heaven. I said to the king, "If it please the king, and if your servant has found favor before you, send me to Judah, to the city of my fathers' tombs, that I may rebuild it." ...So it pleased the king to send me, and I gave him a definite time. And I said to the king, "If it please the king, let letters be given me for the governors... ...And the king granted them to me because the good hand of my God was on me. (Nehemiah 2:4, 5, 6b, 7a and 8b - NASB)

115.

And so, Nehemiah set off for Jerusalem. His first piece of intelligence about the job at hand was the response of the enemies of Israel, who were distressed because someone had the audacity to want to do something good for the Israelites. His second intelligence came when he rode out at night to gauge for himself the extent of the damage to the city wall.

(Leader), I bless you with being vigilant, wise and proactive. As unbelievable as it may seem, there will be those who are not satisfied with your vision of development, restoration and growth. I bless you with ears to hear these rumblings and take note, and with peace to store the information without being gripped by fear.

I bless you with wisdom when to share your vision and with whom. I bless you with demonstrating your passion for and commitment to the vision by not relying on second-hand information only, but putting your feelers out and ensuring you have first-hand knowledge of the task ahead.

When Sanballat the Horonite and Tobiah the Ammonite official heard of it, they were deeply disturbed that a man had come to seek the well-being of the children of Israel. So I came to Jerusalem and was there three days. Then I arose in the night, I and a few men with me; I told no one what my God had put in my heart to do at Jerusalem; nor was there any animal with me, except the one on which I rode. And I went out by night through the Valley Gate to the Serpent Well and the Refuse Gate, and viewed the walls of Jerusalem which were broken down and its gates which were burned with fire. And the officials did not know where I had gone or what I had done; I had not yet told the Jews, the priests, the nobles, the officials, or the others who did the work. (Nehemiah 2:10-13 and 16)

116.

Nehemiah shares his vision with the relevant people. He describes a vision, without sugar-coating it, and appeals to their sense of honour. He encourages them, not with quotes or someone else's good stories, but with his own testimony. Nehemiah is completely authentic in sharing the vision God gave him. The people are enthused. Then the enemies of the nation, Sanballat and his cronies, change tact. They move from being distressed to mocking – it is such a predictable strategy from the enemy to distract us and make us doubt ourselves. Nehemiah will have none of it. He makes a faith declaration about his God, reaffirms the vision and outlines the rights of the enemy – none. (Nehemiah 2:17-20)

(Leader), I bless you with sharing your vision with your sphere of influence in a way suited to your target audience, without compromising the truth. I bless you with clearly communicating the 'what', as well as the 'how', so that everyone will understand their role in attaining the vision. I bless you with being wise as you hear from, or are confronted by your enemies – spiritual, as well as natural. I bless you with discernment to see beyond the mocking, the real motivation, and to not give room for doubt and intimidation.

I bless you with remembering where your vision comes from and that He who promised is faithful. I bless you with repeating the vision as clearly and as often as necessary to encourage your staff or constituents. I bless you with the presence of mind to immediately and visibly refute and reject the enemy's claims.

117.

Chapter three of Nehemiah lists the people who rebuilt the wall and which sections of the wall they worked on. Instead of 32 verses, the whole chapter could have been summarised with, "The Israelites started to rebuild the wall, everyone pitched in except for the nobles of the Tekoites". But, instead, those who laboured are mentioned by name, as well as on which section they worked, in chronological order: an account was kept of who built next to whom and, in some instances, in great detail, for example "… from the angular turning of the wall to the door of the house of … the high priest". In many instances, it is said that the builders built the section of wall in front of their houses. On two occasions, the list mentions the actual occupation of the builders – one, a goldsmith, and another, a perfumer (Nehemiah 3).

(Leader), I bless you with sufficient resources to get the job done. I bless you with conceiving a realistic and practical plan that will attain the vision in the shortest possible time and the most efficient manner. I bless you with knowing who is contributing to the vision (as well as who is slacking) and with acknowledging hard work. The awareness of working towards something great together, is a powerful motivator for you and your people.

While your day might be taken up by many responsibilities that seem far removed from the actual vision, I bless you with knowing in greater detail what is being accomplished, as well as where the bottlenecks are, so that you can celebrate the former and address the latter.

I bless you with a team where everyone contributes – whether by doing what they are supposed to do, or by going the extra mile. By working together, they will all attain the vision. However, team members who do not contribute at all, or less than what they should, drain the energy of the whole team. I bless you with committed, hard-working people. I bless you with stars in your team who have been equipped with many skills, and who are willing and capable to bring their whole set of talents to bear in getting the work done, and not just those particular skills for which they have been appointed.

118.

Sanballat is in a rage. He turns up the heat in his seemingly endless repertoire of derision against the people of Israel. He is joined by Tobiah, who openly questions and insults the builders' abilities and quality of work. Nehemiah reports them to God with some suggestions of what God should do to them. He states the effect of the enemies' taunting on the workers and defends God's honour. The work on the wall continues (Nehemiah 4:1-6).

(Leader), you might never face such extreme intimidation as what Nehemiah faced, but, somewhere along the line, someone will question your abilities and those of your people. I bless you with recognising the motivation behind the criticism and with the resolve to acknowledge, or dismiss its accuracy. I bless you with the freedom to present it before the Lord – it makes you a wise leader, not a weak one. I bless you with being in tune with the mood of the people, so that you can bring alignment or correction, if necessary.

I bless you with the fervour to defend your God and the vision He has given you, not because God needs defending, but because it is one way of honouring His name. I bless you with progress and with a people who will pursue the vision, no matter what. I bless you with a people who have "a heart and mind to work".

119.

Sanballat & co. are very angry. Again. And they have been joined by more enemies of Israel. They planned to attack Jerusalem with the intent to "injure and cause confusion and failure in it". The reaction? It is not only Nehemiah who prays, but also those with him. Secondly, they set a watch against the enemy. But, the strength of the builders is failing, they are surrounded by rubble, and fear the enemy closing in on them. Nehemiah encourages the people; the enemy sees that its plans are known and the work continues (Nehemiah 4:7-15).

(Leader), I bless you with perseverance in times where it seems as if all the odds are against you. I bless you with discernment to identify the strategy of the enemy – it does not only come in the form of verbal or physical abuse, but also in the form of dishonourable behaviour, corruption, lies, intimidation and disunity. I bless you with open communication channels between you and God so that you can hear His warnings; and with the right intelligence at the right time, so that you will be one step ahead of the enemy all the time.

I bless you with people around you who serve the God you serve, the Lord God who is One. I bless you with the right response to the enemy's threats. I bless you with the right words of encouragement for your people – remind them of Him who fights for them, remind them of what is at stake. I bless you with seeing the enemy turning back from you; and with joy at God's salvation.

120.

If ever there was extraordinary commitment to a vision, this was it. One half of the people built, while the other carried the weapons and armour. The leaders were at their posts. Those who built also had their swords at the ready. Nehemiah did the rounds with the trumpeter next to him. He encouraged the people as they worked and ensured that everyone understood the emergency plan. He also went one step further and, leveraging strength in numbers, instructed that everyone should sleep within Jerusalem without common comforts. (Nehemiah 4:6-23).

(Leader), I bless you with being surrounded by people who understand the urgency of the situation you are in. I bless you and your people with the resourcefulness necessary to accomplish the task at hand. I bless you with unity of purpose and focus. I bless you with being a visible leader who takes up their sword alongside the people – showing an interest not only in the people's work, but also in their wellbeing. Like Nehemiah did, I bless you with honouring God for His protection by unashamedly acknowledging it.

I bless you with the wisdom to share the right kind of information with your people at the right time. I bless you with being willing to be uncomfortable for the sake of the vision and your people's safety – when they are required to camp in the city, swords drawn, so should you.

121.

Up until now, Nehemiah's greatest worry had been the enemy nations seeking to destroy the people and Jerusalem. In chapter five, however, Nehemiah also had to contend with unrighteousness in his own nation. As if the rampant poverty was not enough, people were also borrowing money they could not repay, from their Jewish brethren. Interest (which was forbidden by God – see Exodus 22:25) was high and children were being sold into slavery. Nehemiah was very angry about this, but for the first time, he did not act immediately. He thought about the matter first. And then he rebuked those responsible: the nobles and officials (his management team). He did not only tell them that they were doing wrong, but he also connected the dots between their disobedience (not looking after the poor and exacting interest), not fearing (i.e. having reverence for) God and, ultimately, being mocked and criticised by their enemies. He gave a revolutionary instruction that they had to give back what they had taken. Even more revolutionary was the fact that they did! (Nehemiah 5:1-13)

(Leader), I bless you with weathering the storms brought about by enemy agents outside the camp, as well as inside. I bless you with looking after those in your care, and with guarding against, exposing and reproving exploitation.

I bless you with being wise in differentiating between external danger and internal danger. Nehemiah did not have to think how to deal with the external enemies – they were acting in opposition to his God's vision, threatened his people and were, therefore, immediately reported to the Lord.

When the internal danger was exposed, however, he thought about it first – literally, he took counsel with his heart. His people were still acting in opposition to God and he rebuked them for that. He also had to consider corrective measures and bring the nobles and officials to a place of repentance. For that, he needed to consult his heart.

I bless you, (Leader), with using your head and your heart when danger in the camp threatens the vision: Correct that which needs correction and restore what needs restoration.

I bless you with the ability to not only deal with the crude results of disobedience, but to also explain them to your people in the macro context of your environment, so that they will learn wisdom regarding the influence of their actions on the whole company or nation.

122.

Nehemiah had been governor for 12 years. In those 12 years, neither he nor his family had made use of the allowance given to governors by the king. Nehemiah's predecessors "...lived at the expense of the people", and even their servants lorded it over the people. However, Nehemiah's reverent fear of God prevented him from doing the same. Nehemiah still worked on the wall with his servants and he fed 150 people every day at his table, at his own expense. He explained that he did not insist on his rights as governor because the people were already burdened by the tribute due to the king (Nehemiah 5:14-19).

(Leader), I bless you with the courage and determination to swim against the current. I bless you with caring enough about your people and the vision, to be able to reject what the world and society dictate should be yours because of your position, when such entitlements harm your people.

I bless you with a deep understanding in your spirit that your value does not lie in what material wealth your position grants you – you can be stripped of all of this without changing one iota of your value. Also, your authority is not determined by the privileges afforded to those in your position. Your authority is vested in God's establishment of your position.

I bless you with a clear understanding of these truths because when the shaking comes, you will stand on a sure footing, not encumbered and deceived by the temporal security of worldly wealth and status. I bless you with generosity and a willingness to try and lighten the people's burden by doing what is in your power to do.

(Leader), I bless you with receiving from God who sees your acts of kindness, your breaking out of the mould of self-seeking leadership. He will repay you in due time.

123.

Nehemiah's pressure was about to escalate. He had faced enemies to the vision from outside the camp and inside the camp.

Now he was facing opposition from his close circle – his executive team. At the beginning of chapter six, the external enemies changed their strategy. No longer reviling the people, they requested a meeting – possibly for what we would call a round of negotiations. Nehemiah was not fooled. He refused the meeting and stated his commitment to attaining the vision. The enemy then wrote a letter questioning Nehemiah's integrity and loyalty towards the king. Nehemiah called them on their lies and exposed their motives. He asked God to strengthen his hands. Shemaiah, possibly a prophet and someone close to Nehemiah, urged Nehemiah to seek refuge in the temple. Nehemiah recognised the hand of the enemy in this advice, again saw the motive, and brought his enemies to God by name (Nehemiah 6:1-14).

(Leader), I bless you with keeping your eyes on the task at hand and not being distracted by the shenanigans of the enemy. I bless you with wisdom and a healthy dose of realism – if your enemies have harassed you for months and years, the chances of a sudden change of heart without God being behind it are very slim: be on your guard.

I bless you with staying true to the vision, even if years have passed and the initial sense of excitement has made way for the humdrum of getting the job done.

I bless you with keeping a level head when your opposition formalises its complaint against you, i.e. when it moves from hearsay to angry words to official communication. I bless you with stating the facts clearly and succinctly – leave no room for confusion and counterattack.

I bless you, (Leader), with strength to persevere, even when those closest to you have sold you out. I bless you with keeping your ears close to the beating of God's heart and the sound of His counsel to remember His precepts, and not allowing even seemingly good friends to talk you into disobeying His precepts. He is your first responsibility.

I bless you with banishing any trace of fear from your mind or heart – call it by name when it rears its ugly head and reject it. I bless you with sharing your frustrations with God: if you have made Him your number one priority, He will deal with your enemies and will accomplish that which He has ordained for you, no matter what.

124.

The wall is finished. The enemy nations are filled with fear and "…fell far in their esteem", for they saw the work of God (Nehemiah 6:15 and 16).

(Leader), I bless you with that lightheaded, awestruck realisation that your God did it. Through all the effort and danger, He was rooting for you and guarding the vision He had planted in your heart.

I bless you with experiencing His pleasure over you – not because you have accomplished a task, but because you rose up to your God-given potential, standing firm in your faith and on His Word, partnering with the King of kings. I bless you to savour that feeling: let it sink into your heart and build your faith even more, before you move on to the next thing.

Of course, the fact that the wall was finished did not mean that all the work was done. Nehemiah continued to fortify the city and to appoint the right people to guide, teach and minister to the small nation. By God's instruction, he counted the people and then gathered them all together, so that Ezra could read the Torah – the Fatherly instructions for drawing close to God as captured by Moses. The nation wept as they listened to God's Word, which they had not heard, nor obeyed for such a long time. Ezra told them that it was a time for rejoicing, for eating and drinking, and sharing with those who did not have. He confirmed what they had witnessed during the building of the wall – the joy of the Lord was their strength and fortress (Nehemiah 7; 8:1-12).

(Leader), I bless you with gaining new strength to start on the next phase of securing and expanding the vision. I bless you with wisdom to appoint the right people in the right positions – those who can take the vision forward, who will supply the new energy and fresh perspective needed by the 'old guard'. I bless you with knowing the demographics and nuances of your sphere of influence. A company/city/nation with more young people than old, for example; with more parents than single people; with more older men than women, will change the dynamics of operation. It sets the tone of the way you lead.

I bless you with revisiting what God told you, the counsel He has given you, and to share that with your people. I bless you with joy and with celebrating what He has done for you. I bless you with experiencing the joy of the Lord as your strength and stronghold.

126.

The people continued to learn about God's Word – "…to study and understand … divine instruction". They read about the Feast of Booths (Tabernacles) ordained by God to be celebrated in the seventh month and, since it just happened to be the seventh month, they obeyed and celebrated the feast for the first time since Joshua's reign. The Day of Atonement, another of God's set-apart times, followed and the Israelites separated themselves from the foreigners to confess their sins and those of their forefathers, and worship God. Ezra gave a beautiful summary about their God's faithfulness. He reminded them of the God who had brought them out of Egypt, had done great miracles on their behalf, had led them to the country He had bequeathed to them and whom they, the nation, had rejected time and again, while He had remained faithful and ever ready to deliver them when they called to Him (Nehemiah 8-9:38).

(Leader), I bless you with a revelation of God's perfect timing. What you might see as coincidence is, in actual fact, just one of the many fine threads He has been weaving, and is weaving into His universe-sized tapestry.

I bless you with catching a glimpse of His mercy in His timing – bringing you along paths, connecting you with people and opportunities, and showing Himself strong on your behalf.

I bless you with an understanding of His Word – may it come alive to you as something that is more relevant today than

118

the local newspaper. In His Word, you will receive all the guidance you require; in His presence, at His feet, you will have the revelation of what you have read and heard.

I bless you with being obedient to the times He has set apart for you to meet with Him. I bless you with making the time in your busy schedule to meet with Him during these appointed times, as well as those special 'Him-and-you' times that He will ask you for. You will soon find out that these times are invaluable if you want to rule the way you are supposed to, and that they are not burdensome, but life-giving and refreshing.

I bless you with taking stock of your life – how you reign, lead, work, speak, do, live and love. I bless you with a humble heart that is quick to ask forgiveness, if there is any hindrance between you and God. He delights in humility and is eager to bring restoration.

127.

After reading the Word, repenting of their sins and glorifying God, the people recommitted themselves to God and promised to obey His Word according to what Moses had written. The ordinances covered a number of aspects – who they would join; keeping the appointed time of the Sabbath; how to rule over the land; when and how much to give; and how to care for the house of God (Nehemiah 10).

(Leader), I bless you with a heart eager to please God. It is His desire that you do well. Your prosperity in spirit, soul and body brings Him great glory. I bless you with being attentive to His guidance, in terms of who you surround yourself with – both in the course of your tenure and in your personal life. I bless you with honouring Him with your time: this might seem daunting, but you will soon find these times indispensable. I bless you with the heart of a steward, looking after everything over which He has appointed you and causing it to thrive.

I bless you with the pleasure of giving and of doing so in abundance, expecting nothing in return. God loves a cheerful giver and will recompense you in unexpected ways. I bless you with finding a spiritual home or community where you will be blessed and will be a blessing.

128.

Nehemiah 11 and 12 give an account of how the people moved into the city and where they stayed. These chapters mention that the Persian king determined that the singers receive daily provision, and continue in much detail about the Levites and their families. Then the wall was dedicated with great fanfare and jubilation. All the people, the gates and the wall were purified, and at each gate, a procession stopped to give thanks to the Lord: "…the joy of Jerusalem was heard even afar off". More people were appointed over different areas – notably those areas concerning God's instructions to Moses, which had been neglected for so long.

(Leader), I bless you with being surrounded by worshippers, people with a heart after God's presence, and that His presence will fill your constituency, your boardroom, your diary, your home. I bless you with tasting His sweet presence in your own times of worship. As a leader – and, therefore, bound by society's code of conduct for people of stature – this might be new to you: laying your crown aside, and honouring and loving the Creator of the universe(s) and lover of your soul.

I bless you with taking to worshipping your King like a duck to water – may it be said of you that your joy was even heard afar off.

I bless you with seeing how your sphere of influence expands as you realign your life and work with God's requirements. If the example of Nehemiah is anything to go by, being obedient to God leads to job creation! I bless you with celebrating the attainment of the vision and with making celebrations a part of your way of life.

129.

Nehemiah took leave from Jerusalem to return to the king in Persia. He returned to find that the people still had a long way to go in walking in complete obedience; they soon backslid. The priest had prepared a room for a family member – the same Tobiah that had opposed Nehemiah – in the courts of the house of God where the offerings, wine, oil, vessels and tithes for the temple were kept. Nehemiah lost no time in throwing everything out, cleansing the room and restoring it to its proper use. The Levites were not receiving their dues and the Sabbaths were not being kept. In addition, when reading Moses' book, the people found that certain groups were forbidden to come into the assembly of God because they had hired a prophet to curse them years previously. Nehemiah reminded them of how being disobedient to God's Word by marrying heathen women had influenced Solomon and how he had missed the mark because of that (Nehemiah 13).

(Leader), I bless you with leaders serving under you who have a close relationship with God, and in whose care you can entrust the people and the vision when you are not there.

I bless you with a spirit of excellence to ensure that everything concerning your stewardship is done in the proper manner, aligned to God's will. I bless you with never tiring of bringing correction where needed. Compromising on high standards should not even cross your mind.

I bless you with ensuring that everyone in your care receives fair treatment and the remuneration due to them. I bless you with such a walk with God that He will automatically turn every curse spoken against you into a blessing. I bless you with hitting the bull's-eye of leadership because you are faithful to God's ordinances for holy living.

130.

So much more could be said about and learnt from Nehemiah. We end this chapter by looking at his own prayers for himself to God (Nehemiah 4:4, 5; 5:19; 13:14, 22, 31).

(Leader), I bless you with God hearing your prayers regarding your enemies. I bless you with God earnestly remembering all the good you have done for your people. I bless you with God remembering your good deeds for His house and His service. I bless you with experiencing God's mercy and loving-kindness. I bless you, (Leader), with God imprinting you on His heart.

Chapter 14: Praying the Psalms

Introduction

Much has been written about praying the Word. If we are to pray to our Father in heaven and ask that His will be done on earth as it is in heaven, as instructed by Jesus in Matthew 6:10, how will we know His will if we do not know His Word?

His Word gives us so much insight and revelation about what He values and His Kingdom principles – if only we would start valuing it, not as a novel of historic interest, but as a living and relevant covenant declaration stipulating how we should draw near to Him and how to prepare as the Bride of Messiah!

And even if we know His Word, how can we be obedient, if we regard His Word as something written for another people in ancient times? He has not changed His mind about anything written in His Word. If we can train ourselves, under the leading of the Holy Spirit, to appropriate what is written in Scripture to our daily lives and current circumstances, much will be accomplished.

The book of Psalms is an oasis of authentic expression of the relationship between man and God. It lifts us up and encourages; it helps us to praise and worship the King of kings when our own words are lacking; it puts into words what our deepest desires for and from the Lord struggle to articulate.

It is also a book full of the golden nuggets of God's Kingdom principles. In this chapter, we use a few Psalms, aligned with the leadership blessings in the previous chapters, to pray over or bless a leader.

∼✑∽

Press in

131.

Legitimising leadership

(Leader), I declare Psalm 75 over your life. I bless you with declaring God's wondrous works. I bless you with being aligned to His perfect timing. I bless you with overcoming any temptation to boast because of your position. God decides to put down one and exalt another – I bless you to draw comfort from that because you have been chosen by God, but to also heed the warning inherent in God's sovereign decision-making. I bless you with singing praises to the God of Jacob and with Him lifting you up, His righteous one.

132.

Knowing God

(Leader), listen to the promises in Psalm 4. I bless you with the God of your righteousness answering you when you call. I bless you with experiencing His grace when He hears your prayer and allays your distress. I bless you with the certainty that because you know Him, He hears your call and because of your trust in Him, He will lift up the light of His countenance upon you. I bless you with receiving joy from the Lord, with peace and with dwelling in safety.

Righteous leadership

(Leader), Psalm 1 pits righteous leadership against wicked leadership. I bless you with being in the camp of the former. I bless you with receiving the blessing from God for not walking in the counsel of the wicked, and not standing in the path of sinners or being associated with mockers. I bless you with delighting in and meditating on the Torah of God, His instructions for us to get to know Him. I bless you with being like a fruitful tree planted by water, ever prospering. I bless you with being able to stand in the judgement – if you walk in righteousness, you will not be like the wicked who perish.

Wisdom

(Leader), read Psalm 37 – again and again: it is a leadership code of conduct in its own right. I bless you with not worrying about, nor envying the wicked.

I bless you with trusting in God and doing good; cultivating faithfulness; delighting yourself in God; receiving from Him the desires of your heart; committing your way to Him; resting in Him and waiting for Him; ceasing from anger and revenge; inheriting the land and enjoying great prosperity because of your humility; hearing the Lord laughing at your enemies; seeing Him fighting on your behalf; being sustained by God and not knowing shame; being gracious and giving; walking on the paths He has directed you; knowing that God holds your hand;

taking comfort in Him never forsaking you; uttering wisdom and speaking justice; holding the Law of God in your heart; having a sure footing wherever you go; remaining blameless before God; being known as a person of peace; and forever taking your refuge in the Lord.

135.

Stewardship

(Leader), I bless you with fearing the Lord and finding pleasure in His commandments, so that you will be fruitful in every way. I bless you with wealth and riches governed by righteousness. I bless you with being gracious and compassionate; with giving freely and being true in judgement. I bless you with never being shaken and with being remembered. I bless you with being fearless, trusting God and enjoying the blessing that comes from giving to the poor. I bless you with seeing your God act on your behalf because you are a trustworthy steward of all He has given you. (*Based on Psalm 112*)

136.

Behaviour

(Leader), Psalm 15 describes those who may freely approach God. I bless you with these characteristics, as they will transform your leadership behaviour into something that gives life and honours God. I bless you with walking in integrity; working righteousness; loving the truth; guarding your words; doing no evil to anyone; hating gossip; honouring and fearing

God; foregoing interest on loans; and refusing to take and give bribes. I bless you with never being shaken.

137.

Blessed by God

(Leader), Psalm 67 confirms that God delights in blessing us. I bless you with this truth. May God be gracious to you and bless you, may His face shine upon you. I bless you with making known God's way on earth, so that His name may be praised wherever you go. I bless you with being guided by the Lord. I bless you with having a heart that overflows with praise for Him, especially as you see your fruit increase in your sphere of influence. I bless you with being blessed by God as a testimony to the reverence due to Him.

138.

Equipped by God

(Leader), Psalm 65 speaks about God's favour on the earth and man. He has prepared everything in time for us to enjoy. I bless you with delighting in the Lord's diverse provision: hearing your prayers; forgiving your transgressions; and bringing you near to Him to enjoy the welfare and beauty of His home. I bless you with trusting Him as the mighty one who establishes the mountains, reigns over the seas, orders the sun to come up and go down, and prepares the earth to bring forth every good thing.

I bless you with knowing that, if He takes this much effort to equip the earth, He will do a great deal more for you, who was made in His likeness.

139.

Encouraged by God

(Leader), I bless you with devouring the truths in Psalm 119. I encourage you to know that, when your soul is distressed, He will revive you. I bless you with Him teaching and helping you to understand His precepts. I bless you with meditating on His grandeur, with being strengthened when you are grieving. I bless you with walking in truth and being faithful. I bless you with holding on to God's testimonies and His faithfulness. I bless you with having your heart enlarged, so that you can follow His direction. (*vv. 25-32*)

140.

Guided by God

(Leader), I bless you with accepting the Lord as your Shepherd and Provider. I bless you with following Him to restful and beautiful places. I bless you with the Lord restoring your soul and guiding you in the ways of righteousness. I bless you with being fearless because He is with you to guide you and comfort you. I bless you with knowing that He has your back; He has established you and He makes your cup overflow. I bless you with His goodness and kindness following you wherever you go. (*Based on Psalm 23*)

Right counsel

(Leader), I bless you with seeing from God's perspective. He sees everything and hears everything being said by leaders behind closed doors and on public platforms. He laughs at them. I bless you with not being in the same company as those who will hear Him speaking to them in His anger, terrifying them with His fury. Do not be in their counsel and receive no counsel from them.

I bless you with receiving counsel from the Lord and with being generous in asking – even to include nations in your request. I bless you with discernment; worship God, rejoice in Him, revere His Son, so that He does not become angry and you do not lose your refuge. (*Based on Psalm 2*)

Leaving a legacy

(Leader), I bless you with God speaking to you, helping you, giving you instruction. I bless you with being fervent in your estimation of God's honour. I bless you with knowing God as your strength and shield, as your Help in ruling in your position. I bless you with His defence and salvation, and with Him blessing His inheritance over which you have been appointed. I bless you to walk in the footsteps of the shepherd, so that your legacy will bring Him praise. (*Based on Psalm 28*)

Example of godly leadership

(Leader), I bless you with seeing God's salvation in difficult times and with being guided by Him in responding to those who criticise you. I bless you with trusting in God's Word and with waiting for Him to instruct you. I bless you with walking in liberty because you seek to do His commandments. I bless you with not being ashamed of God before others. I bless you to delight in His instruction, and to meditate on it and how it relates to your position. (*Based on Psalm 119:41-48*)

Chapter 15: The Lord bless you

Introduction

God's Word is powerful. It is relevant. It is life-changing. It is an epic of a passionate, loving, holy Father's covenant to redeem His Son's fallen Bride. The actors are prepared, the scenes change precisely on cue, the ending is cast in stone – and it's a glorious one.

In His wisdom, He has made us co-authors. What are we writing? Are we using the tools He has given us to frustrate and confuse the enemy's hijacking of the plot, or are we just going with the flow? Are we functioning in our authority to make major edits, pre-approved by the Author, or are we so brainwashed by the same rubbishy storyline that we think this is how it should be?

Leadership is from God. He tells us to pray for those in authority, if we want to live in peace. He gives us the precise coordinates to make sure we hit the mark in prayer. He gives us His example and His heart to bless – to 'release from restrictions and limitations… to infuse the object of blessing with unlimited potential and empowerment'. What we need to do is to obey.

Let's partner with Him in transforming our leadership, in supporting those who have to make the difficult decisions for the good of a nation or a company.

Let's exercise our faith and please God; let's believe Him when He says that He is with us every step of the way – that we have His full endorsement for bringing Kingdom principles to bear on earth.

We started with the Priestly Blessing of Numbers 6. It seems fitting to end with it. However, this version is an interpretation of Numbers 6:24-26 as transcribed by a Jewish teacher looking at the original picture language of Hebrew, as well as the Jewish cultural frame of reference, knowledge and experience of God.

This blessing is what our God wants for you – this is what He pronounces as He bends towards us, lifting our heads with His hand and smiling into our faces.

❦

Press in

144.

May Adonai bless you, release you from restrictions and limitation, and infuse you with unlimited potential and empowerment. May Adonai zealously cherish, diligently defend, guard, keep watch over, protect, treasure and save you, and make your divine destiny His highest priority.

May Adonai's face shine upon you which is the illuminating power of His face as warming energy, healing energy, soothing energy, restorative energy, constantly renewing energy, empowering energy, and shower you with grace.

May Adonai give you whatever it takes to bring you to the point of full covenant participation and enjoyment, and to the fulfilment of your destiny.

May Adonai lift up His countenance upon you to transcend the flames and to experience spiritual reality as it is. And may He give you wholeness, wellness, security, purposeful living, joy, abundant provision, peace, completion, harmony, safety and covenant enjoyment.

(With permission from William G. Bullock, Rabbi's Son)